M000073507

MULTI

THE CHEMISTRY OF CHURCH DIVERSITY

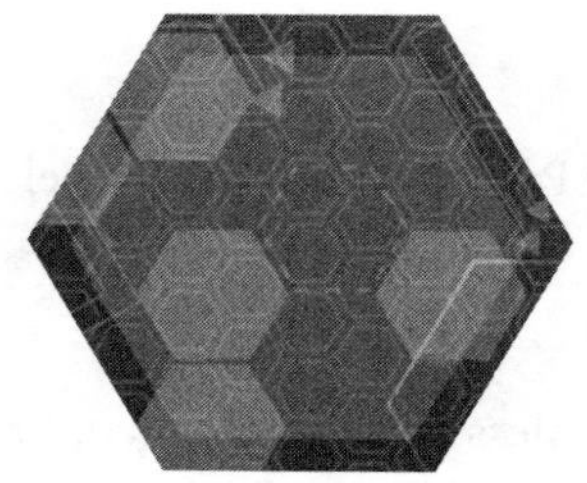

PAUL NIXON

Foreword by Eric H. F. Law

The Pilgrim Press, 700 Prospect Avenue, Cleveland, Ohio 44115
thepilgrimpress.com
© 2019 by Paul Nixon

Scripture quotations, unless otherwise noted, are from the New Revised Standard Version of the Bible, © 1989 by the Division of Christian Education of the National Council of the Churches of Christ in the United States of America, and are used by permission. Changes have been made for inclusivity.

Printed in the United States of America on acid-free paper

23 22 21 20 19 5 4 3 2 1

Cataloging-in-Publication Data can be found online at the Library of Congress. ISBN 978-0-8298-2047-8

CONTENTS

Foreword . . . vii

Preface: Our Journey into the Century of Multi . . . xi

1 Multivalence . . . 1

2 The Practices . . . 17

3 The Capacities: Multicultural . . . 34

4 The Capacities: Multifaith . . . 60

5 The Capacities: Multilocational . . . 71

6 The Leader Team . . . 91

7 The Possibilities . . . 113

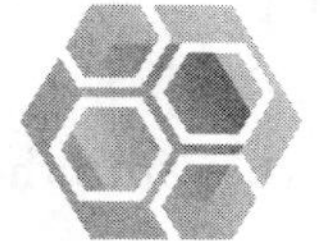

Foreword

"A multicultural community must foster the commitment to accept and work through the existence of more than one cultural framework within the community. We must continuously affirm that not only are there culture differences, but that these differences must always be understood totally within the context of the relevant culture."[1] Twenty years ago, I wrote this challenge in *The Bush Was Blazing But Not Consumed*. This description of the commitment to cultural pluralism was an unrealized vision for many church communities back then, as it is today, because so many of our church communities were still in denial of the multicultural nature of society. Some communities were actually fighting against such a multi-contextual reality by putting down and pushing away differences. Even when church communities could see, hear, and smell the differences that existed in their neighborhoods, they tried to minimize them by emphasizing our sameness and ignoring our differences.

---

1. See Eric H. F. Law, *The Bush Was Blazing But Not Consumed* (St. Louis: Chalice Press, 1996), 67.

Somehow, many churches were stuck with the idea that churches should be "mono"—monolingual, mono-musical taste, mono-theological, mono-liturgical, mono-site, mono-time, mono-ethnic, etc. and then they proceeded to stuff the multi-nature of our world into their mono-structure of their churches. Moving from this mono to a multi mindset requires at least two, if not three, fundamental paradigm shifts—from denial-defense-minimization to acceptance of the multi-reality.[2]

Even the paradigm of language needs to shift. As I was writing the above paragraph, I realized that the spellcheck in my computer accepted many of the words that I had to hyphenate in the past such as multicultural and intercultural. I was never a great speller, so the spellcheck function of my first personal computer was a godsend in 1986 when I was working on my first book. However, every time I typed in the word multicultural or intercultural, spellcheck would not accept it as a real word. I finally settled with hyphenating these words so I didn't have to see so many red lines in my document.

Human languages are only approximations of reality. What we experience of our environment, and whatever language we use to describe reality, is never quite complete or adequate. Conditioned by the communities in which we are raised, we often see what we want to see. When we write down our limited description, we simply assume it is accurate and true. Furthermore, we may strive to force reality to conform to what we think it is. Since we don't have words for every experience and we don't

---

2. For a full description of the different stages of the Developmental Model of Intercultural Sensitivity, see Milton J. Bennett, *Basic Concepts of Intercultural Communication* (Boston: Intercultural Press, 2013), 83–103.

experience all of reality, we treat the limits of language as unimportant and therefore, we ignore them.

Generations of writers who have struggled to describe reality as it is and not as we think it should be, have been inventing new words to open readers' minds to perceive reality. Multicultural, multiracial, multiethnic, and multilingual are all words that are accepted by spellcheck now, and it is a sign that our society is slowly moving toward the acceptance of our multi-contextual reality, thanks to writers who started hyphenating or creating words that they considered essential to describe our reality.

Paul Nixon is one of these writers who find new words to describe the real reality. He invites us to enter into the century of multi: multi-lingual, multi-narrative, multi-theological, multi-liturgical, multi-ethnic, multi-generational, multi-site, and more. What if multi is the norm? What if multi is how God had always created this world? What if multi is how God intended for us to embody God's presence in the world?

Many writers would stop at describing this real reality that has always been there and leave the practical solutions of addressing the problems, issues, and concerns raised by accepting this reality to others, but not Paul Nixon. With his extensive experience in working with local churches, he shows us how to minister faithfully in this multi-reality. He shows us what leadership skills are needed and what organizational structures are required to engage faithfully this acknowledged reality.

"We speak of pluralism as if it is something new that we have to contend with in the twenty-first century. But pluralism—and its diversity of experiences, assumptions, perceptions, frameworks, beliefs and values—has been around for a long time. It was around during Jesus' early ministry and certainly during the formation of the early church. The early Christian church leaders had to address issues raised by pluralism that existed among the believers. Read Acts and you will see how the apostles faced pluralism head-on as they moved the Christian faith beyond the boundary of the Jewish community."[3] Even the inclusion of four Gospels in the biblical canon reflect the early church leaders' struggle to find ways to be faithfully multi.

More than twenty years ago, I challenged our churches to make a commitment to cultural pluralism in order to build a faithful interculturally competence community. However, there has been limited number of books, workshops and resources developed over the years that actually assist church communities to move toward this mission. Paul Nixon's book *Multi* is a great addition to these growing resources. Read it, allow it to challenge you, and, most importantly, let it to guide you into actions that transform your way of doing ministry in this century of multi.

Eric H. F. Law
October 15, 2018

---

3. See Eric H. F. Law, *The Word at the Crossings: Living the Good News in a Multicontextual Community* (St. Louis: Chalice Press, 2004), 27.

Preface

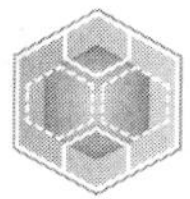

Our Journey into the Century of Multi

In the final year of the final decade of the last millennium, my church was busy getting ready to launch our second campus. Not everyone at Gulf Breeze United Methodist Church was happy about this. The very idea that a congregation could be, geographically speaking, both *here* and *there* was a brain twister for some.

Their paradigm of church was a single, homogeneous worship community where:

- familiar faces showed up in familiar places so that everyone could physically see everyone else, same time, same place, week after week;
- we could watch the kids grow up and the grandparents grow old across the years, just like in a small village;

- there was enough cultural sameness that we could all laugh at the same jokes on the front end of the sermon and appreciate the same music.

The fact that our church was now gathering in four worship services held at different times was unnerving. That we had recently split into two distinctive liturgical styles within the community further contributed to a sense of uneasiness. The bandwidth of human diversity was widening at Gulf Breeze Church. It didn't feel like a cozy church family anymore in the way a lot of folks had once experienced.

But now the proposal that we would launch a fifth service at a second location eight miles away—simultaneous with one of our existing services—this was too much. Even as people had begun to think of church in ways that transcended a single worship community gathered all together in one time and place, they had shifted to another assumption: that a parish is defined by a single facility, one church house in which many different activities can occur.

The second campus launched quite well (except for a problem on opening day when the toilets did not flush). We gathered hundreds of new persons from the get-go, about half of whom were either new to organized church or returning after a long time-out. There were beautiful stories—so many stories of lives blessed and transformed. Most of the contrarians shrugged off the paradigm-disconnect and joined in celebration that God was working so powerfully in our community.

Several years later, just as they were getting used to life in a church that met in two places, we began plans to add a third worship location and to shift from a single pastor model to three co-pastors. Three campuses turned out to be harder than two, with the necessary internal shifts and the expanding human diversity. It all seemed sheer madness to twentieth-century church sensibilities. It was something that could not possibly work. And yet, so long as the pastors stayed on the same page, it worked quite well.[4]

We had entered the "century of multi." And though we were fixated on the novelty of church in multiple locations, we were stumbling into something bigger than our church's relationship to noncontiguous real estate—something far bigger! The real revolution was our significant increase in the scope of human diversity that God was holding together in one multisite congregation.

All over North America, we are witnessing a revolutionary shift in what Martin Luther King Jr. called "the most segregated hour in Christian America,"[5] as more faith communities blend cultural tribes and lifestyle groups into a common life. This multi movement promises to powerfully shape twenty-first-century Christianity, in which the multisite phenomenon will be simply a footnote in a larger movement of God. We are witnessing a twenty-first-century iteration of Pentecost: the rise of the multi church.

At the time that we opened our Community Life Center, in 1999, there were around a hundred multisite churches in existence across America, most of those nondenominational. Two decades later, there are thousands of such congregations, and they come in all sizes and denominational traditions. It did not take long for entrepreneurial church leaders to discover the wisdom of doing ministry in multiple places as one church. In fact,

---

4. For more on this, see my first book, *Fling Open the Doors: Giving the Church Away to the Community* (Nashville: Abingdon Press, 2002).

5. Martin Luther King Jr., *Meet the Press* telecast, NBC, April 17, 1960.

it is now the most dependable way to plant a Christian community presence in a new location or in a location where an earlier faith community has run out of steam. What seemed crazy twenty years ago has become quite common.

During 2009–11, Christie Latona and I studied churches in North America and Asia that were thriving in their initiatives to start new things for new people. The results of this study led to the Readiness 360 Project,[6] by which we sought to measure essential aspects of a church's culture that are highly relevant to its ability to do multiministry. (We were also trying to figure out why some mother churches eat their young!) We identified four key areas of local church culture relevant to multiplication and diversification of ministry, in addition to pastoral leadership. They are (1) intensity of spiritual practice and experience, (2) relational health within the congregation and between the church and its neighbors, (3) alignment with the church's mission, and (4) cross-cultural capacities.[7] This fourth item came a bit as a surprise, especially since we saw so many multisite churches following a franchise formula for each new place they opened. We discovered that while they may standardize certain aspects of their operation, they typically are also willing to dance with the idiosyncrasies of each local culture—to contextualize the gospel. This dance gives such churches a can-do flexibility that is lacking in many established congregations.

Most churches will choose to keep their main operations on one piece of property—and yet in this century of multi, they will

---

6. See "Readiness 360: Multiply Your Impact" at www.readiness360.org.

7. For a deeper exploration of an organization's intercultural capacity, see a tool called *Intercultural Development Inventory* (idiinventory.com).

still be challenged to a deep rethink as we move beyond assumed norms of homogeneity in church life and in culture to a world that runs multi—in varied ways. The issues of multi are almost inescapable for us.

A multi church is a congregation committed to embracing a wider range of human diversity as a part of its vision and practice. This diversity is nurtured at every level of its life, from the leader table to the worship crowd to the ministry teams. This commitment is driven more by love for our neighbors than by a quest for institutional survival amid changing demographics—although both motivations are alive in most multi churches!

This book is an exploration of how diverse people partner together to be church.

As we think together in these pages about the capacities needed for a multi ministry, three notes of caution are in order.

First, no church lives equally into all the possibilities of multi, nor is this necessary. So, if you hit upon a section in the pages ahead that pushes you to overload, relax. Panic is not helpful, and it can close down your openness to critical ideas that apply very readily to your church in the near term. The western world is quite diverse in terms of life experiences and worldview—and we can easily find ourselves polarizing around this or that. One of the promises of a deeply multi church is that we may be able to develop a greater resistance to polarization in the years ahead. The way your church lives into multi will be different than mine! And this is good.

Second, for a congregation to live well in a multi sort of way, there must a coherence of identity and narrative that binds it together amid the challenges of different life experiences, tastes, tribal alliances, outlooks, and so forth. This book is not an invitation to a free-for-all, where one idea is as good as another—there has never been a thriving spiritual movement that lacked an energizing core of commonality. Diversity will be experienced as a blessing only when we are cognizant of that which we hold in common. Lovett Weems says, "Rather than inhibiting diversity, a shared core identity makes greater diversity possible."[8] The Christ event will remain at the center of history for Christians, through it all. Churches that lose their Christology tend to evaporate.

Third, the ways that churches define their identity and narrative will vary from one church to the next. This in itself is nothing new in America, where we have lived with substantial religious pluralism for a long time.[9]

I'm glad you are reading this book! The first chapter (just ahead) builds the foundation for all that follows. It is based upon a metaphor that might take you back to high school chemistry. Fear not! I'm betting you will enjoy the next chapter more than you did high school chemistry.

---

8. Lovett Weems, "General Conference is Broken; Annual Conferences Are Not." churchleadership.com, April 9, 2019.

9. Beth Estock and Paul Nixon, *Weird Church: Welcome to the Twenty-First Century* (Cleveland: Pilgrim Press, 2016). In the opening pages of our book *Weird Church*, Beth Estock and I offered Spiral Dynamics theory as a tool for reframing the cultural challenges facing twenty-first-century churches. We felt it is important to move beyond trying to explain everything according to generational tastes or according to some grand (and simplistic) liberal-conservative continuum. Human beings are infinitely more complex and more interesting than any cultural theory—but I think that Spiral Dynamics offers a more expansive framework for processing cultural change and conflict than any other that has come along. I will not rehash the first twelve pages of *Weird Church* here, but if you are not familiar with Spiral Dynamics, I would recommend picking up a copy of that book.

1

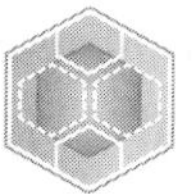

MULTIVALENCE

A few years back, I coached a pastor by the name of Julian Davies. Julian had been Distinguished University Professor of Chemistry and Associate Dean for the Natural Sciences and Mathematics at the University of Toledo (Ohio). In the middle of an agnostic adulthood and at the height of an academic career, Julian met Christ in a very personal way. God then called him to pastoral ministry. Off to seminary he went. Upon graduation, he went back to Toledo to plant University Church adjacent to the school where he had previously taught.

When I began exploring multivalence as a metaphor for twenty-first-century ministry, I knew I needed to catch up with Julian. I am certainly not a chemist, though I enjoyed two years of high school chemistry and even made a pile of aspirin once in lab. I needed to test my understanding of valence with an expert.

Beyond catching up personally, Julian gave me a little chemistry refresher.

Valence refers to the bonding capabilities of a chemical element and the ease with which an element gives or receives energy from another element (synergy). Chemists assign a valence number to elements depending on how many different elements they can bond with simultaneously. Hydrogen, the simplest of all elements, has a valence of one. This means it can bond with one thing at a time. Give it some oxygen and the hydrogen will bond and happily form water—a very stable substance.

Some elements have a valence of zero. These are called noble gases: neon and helium. They are not looking to bond with anything. This makes them very stable to work with but also a bit boring.[10] Another way of saying it: these elements typically remain in a state of inertia. They don't do anything with other elements. Nothing happens between them and their neighbors. No synergy can be found here. Julian refers to these elements as having a "closed shell." Not only do they never come out of the house, there is no door or space for anything to get in.

Multivalence, in contrast, means that there are multiple possibilities built into the essence of an element for bonding with other elements. An atom with a capacity for partnering with other kinds of atoms is multivalent. The greater the number of elements that an atom can partner with, the higher valence number chemists assign to that atom. Carbon, for example, has a valence of four—meaning that it can bond with up to four different elements simultaneously to create complex and interesting molecules. (Molecules are simply partnerships of atoms.) When certain elements

---

10. Of course, neon lit up the original Vegas Strip—which was anything but boring—reminding us that even when we do not bond readily with other entities, we can still bring light and joy to the world!

bond easily with the carbon atom, we say there is affinity between the elements. Multivalent elements may have far-ranging affinities.

Now, it so happens that carbon-based molecules form the basis for the creation of all life. If not for the multivalence of carbon, no life would exist! This alone offers us a clue that multivalence is a very good characteristic for those of us who want to lead life-giving churches. It is not only carbon's valance (four) that makes it such a special element, but also the fact that when carbon bonds, it has a habit of using all of its electrons constructively in the bond. No electrons are left mischievously wandering loose to create havoc and repel the bond. This is called covalent bonding—every electron in the game! (We will return to this point in the pages ahead.) Because carbon bonds so readily, without electron resistance, it can form the basis of enormously complex molecules: hence the possibility of life.

In the world of medicine, the term multivalence is sometimes used with reference to pharmaceuticals. It's the same concept, except it relates simply to how easily the molecule of a particular medicine can bond with antibodies. A high valence in a medicine means that it possesses more molecular ports for bonding with other molecules in the human body, relevant to healing disease.

In the world of art, multivalence refers to an artistic work that can be interpreted in different ways, or that can provide meaning in different contexts. People are able to latch onto the art for multiple reasons. Work that is deemed to be great art is often multivalent; many people connect to it and in varied ways. Scripture is one example of multivalent art, and the implications of this for multivalent churches are considered in chapter 3.

In the world of Christianity, we all know churches that have a valence of zero; they are content to keep their life mostly in-house. They may offer wonderful ministries of kindness toward their neighbors (or not), but it's hard to bond with them in deeper relationship. Their understanding of mission rarely if ever extends to inviting folks home for dinner. More commonly, I see churches with a valence of one: they are designed to catch one kind of fish, to reach and connect with one culture of people. A multivalent church, however, develops capacities for partnering with a diverse array of people.

In 1978 the Lausanne Committee for World Evangelization famously quoted Donald McGavran as saying that people "like to become Christians without crossing racial, linguistic or class barriers."[11] In other words, people prefer to do spirituality within their native cultural context, in ways that feel organic to their sensibilities as opposed to ways that feel forced or alien. This principle of homogeneity is often misinterpreted as an endorsement of the monocultural church. In fact, McGavran was a proponent for the creation of many different kinds of culturally homogeneous cells and churches as a practical matter for reaching new populations. When creating faith community with new groups of people, the idea is to take their cultural context seriously—and not simply to impose the practices, music, or key theological metaphors of another (often European-heritage) culture. New music, new traditions, new ministry practices, new insights into the gospel—all of this is made possible by taking each culture or subculture seriously. McGavran believed that, by creating different kinds of cells, the church could connect more easily

---

11. Lausanne Committee for World Evangelization, *Lausanne Occasional Paper: The Pasadena Consultation: Homogeneous Unit Principle,* section 3, "The Homogeneous Unit Principle and Evangelism," 1978, www.lausanne.org.

with an ever expanding variety of people, specializing in endless cultural contexts and life affinities.

But a starting place in mission (a particular culture or affinity group) should not be assumed to be the ending place! Just because churches can most easily reach persons within a specific cultural context should in no way lead us to conclude that the church should stop there. What is the point of leaving people segregated from one another in the family of God? Following Jesus is inevitably a journey into the discovery of one's connectedness with all of humanity and all of creation. If Dr. McGavran were with us today, I have no doubt he would be an enthusiastic proponent of a multivalent ministry. Multivalent churches must pay attention to affinities and issues of homo- and heterogeneity.[12]

The Lausanne statement eloquently said as much:

> It seems probable that, although there were mixed Jewish-Gentile congregations, there were also homogeneous Jewish congregations (who still observed Jewish customs) and homogeneous Gentile congregations (who observed no Jewish customs). Nevertheless, Paul clearly taught them that they belonged to each other in Christ, that they must welcome one another as Christ had welcomed them (compare Romans 15:7), and that they must respect one another's consciences, and not offend one another. He publicly rebuked Peter in Antioch for withdrawing from table fellowship with Gentile believers, and argued that his action was a denial of the truth of the gospel, that is, of

12. See also Michael Moynagh, *Church in Life: Innovation, Mission, and Ecclesiology*, chapter 11: "Affinity Group Theology," (London: SCM Press, 2017), 219–36.

> the justification of all believers (whether Jews or Gentiles) by grace through faith (compare Galatians 2:11–16). This incident and teaching should be taken as a warning to all of us of the seriousness of permitting any kind of apartheid in the Christian fellowship.[13]

A multivalent church is able to connect with diverse groups of people because it crafts particular ways and places for connection with specific populations. Customized points of connection make diversity possible!

No church can or should reach every kind of person or excel in every kind of outreach ministry. The accommodations that would be necessary to reach everyone could destroy any vestige of coherence and identity within the congregation. That would be a disaster. As my friend Julian reflected on his church, he said they try to keep focused on a couple areas of ministry in the community (food and kids), so that they don't disperse their energy beyond what they can do well. He reflected on this and said, "This would give us a valence of two." If he were to evaluate University Church with the exercise at the end of this chapter, he might find the valence is indeed a bit higher than two, but an unlimited valence is specifically something that he would seek to avoid. It is beyond what his church can handle. Thriving churches will often work to increase their valence, but only to the point that they can handle the complexity while retaining their internal coherence. Uranium has a valance of six, but it's highly unstable and could blow up more than just the garage if handled improperly.

---

13. Lausanne Committee, *Lausanne Occasional Paper 1*, section 5, "The Church, the Churches and the Homogenous Unit Principle."

Even multivalent atoms, as they bond with others, reach a point of stability where they have no further capacity for bonding with anything else. Within these molecules (partnering arrangements of atoms), the constituent atoms have bonded well with each other, so well that there is no additional capacity for bonding with anything else. Therefore, it can be said that such molecules also have a "closed shell." They cannot be stretched further, except under special conditions.[14] This points toward an excellent reason for planting new congregations—so that churches can expand the variety of people included in ministry without creating a pressure-cooker situation within a single congregation.[15]

It is important, as we learn from this metaphor of nature and as we appreciate the value of multivalence, that we note the limits that nature observes. In church terms, while a valence of zero is not very promising for the mission, a very high valence can present its own set of risks. A high valence church must work to stay remarkably aligned and must constantly nurture very high trust within the body. When we see (or lead) a church with a high valence, we should be on the lookout for threats to the church's unity and continued thriving. There may even come points where we choose to let some parts of the molecule spin off. To go back to the metaphor of the organic (carbon-based) molecules—even though they can grow to great complexity, they also have the

14. The gospel itself can create special conditions, at times acting as a catalyst that expands a community's valence. Brenda Salter McNeil made this point with great passion on April 30, 2018, during her plenary at the Large Church Initiative gathering in San Diego.

15. The same might also be said of creating new denominations—we do not have to view schism as failure—it may also be a mark of widening inclusivity in the global body of Christ.

capacity to divide and multiply. By releasing one another at certain points, the growth of a larger organism continues.[16]

If we persist in bonding an ever expending list of elements (or people groups) together without paying attention to basic issues of stability, we will blow up the lab. That is just how it works.

Based upon the typical metrics of membership, weekly participation, and financial giving, it is sometimes hard to tell which churches have the sort of robustness that will see them through the next twenty years. Sometimes I see churches with an aging membership and overall net income shrinking that also show signs of a surging renewal of life. The surge may not yet be enough to outpace the loss of older members and lost annual pledges. But the surge is a sign that God is doing a new thing in that church—and that the church has a good future—perhaps downsized, but still, a future!

Many critical issues of church health are not highlighted on the various congregational management dashboards that we see across the land. First, the Readiness 360 inventory helps me to look under the hood to see a variety of factors that can be hard to quantify: relating to spiritual practices, relationships, alignment, and cultural openness.

In addition, here are ten questions that I ask when I am consulting onsite with a congregation, as I am seeking to discover their future prognosis:

- Is there a significant prayerful, contemplative practice among the leaders in the church?

16. It is unhelpful to view such releasing as a failure. It is a part of ministry multiplication. God has never revealed any design whereby all of the church was to be structurally and organizationally connected.

- If we were to come up with an expanded ministry game plan in this place, could the pastor (and lead team) quarterback it?
- Does the church have an organized plan or process for helping its people deepen their relationship to God and to live out the core values of their faith?[17]
- And are at least half the regular participants in the church participating in the aforementioned plan or process?
- *Is the church committed to loving its neighbors in specific, tangible ways that rally the energy of its members and that build trust and solidarity with folks beyond its bounds, especially with those who suffer?*
- *How many new groups, teams, circles, services (etc.) did the church start this year?*
- *Is the participation level of children and teens growing?*
- *Is the church making intentional strides forward to engage people digitally?*[18]
- Are new people regularly, steadily signing on to join the community? Are there new members, new regular participants?[19]

---

17. Sometimes such a plan for intentional spiritual development of people within a church is called a Discipleship Pathway.
18. This relates to the number of monthly hits on the church website, as well as the numbers of people who move from website engagement to participation in some other aspect of the church's ministry. If the church is webcasting its worship service(s) or developing online studies, are they quickly moving to the place where the web participation for these things exceeds the number of people who gather in a physical building? Digital ministry competency is an increasing focus of our consulting work at the Epicenter Group.
19. Notice that we are just looking at new life entering into the church system this year—not the accumulated membership totals from across the years.

- Are a significant percentage of the adults joining the community by profession of faith,[20] as opposed to simply transferring from another church?

The first two questions have to do specifically with the leaders. The next two have to do with the spiritual journey of the people within the congregation (including the leaders). Four of the ten questions (in *italics*) have to do with multivalence. These questions relate to relationship building between the church and the wider community, so that there can be more ports of entry for people to get in to the church. The last two questions have to do with the fruit of the ministry, specifically related to how many folks actually got in last year. If a church is in good shape on most of the these fronts, their future is bright!

I watch for the following signs of multivalence:

- Strategies and practices of building relationships with neighbors. Without trust, people aren't stepping into the life or worship gatherings of any church. Without relationship, there is no trust. So what are we doing to make new friends as church communities? How are we seriously listening to and partnering with our neighbors, creating entryway experiences for our neighbors so that trust increases?
- Steady creation of new groups and gatherings at *different times* and in *different places*. New groups are easier to join; groups in existence for more than a year are often nearly impossible to join. A lot of people in our communities have

20. Profession of faith means different things from church to church. I am simply looking at people who were not a part of an organized faith community in the several years prior to joining the life of this one.

A FEW TOPICS *NOT* ON MY TOP-TEN LIST

- How good a preacher is the pastor?
- How good is the music?
- How is the building or the parking?
- What is the per capita giving?
- Is membership growing?

These are not irrelevant; they are simply secondary issues. The first two items are quite subjective. And I have seen plenty of churches with stellar worship services sink into oblivion. Buildings can be replaced and new sites can be added. Generosity always follows discipleship; I have yet to see a church of faithful people anywhere on the planet who could not find an effective ministry approach within their financial means. (I have seen a few who quit or closed because they were unwilling to rethink the way they depended upon high-dollar items.) And the membership roll is often so bloated with names from yesteryear that the total number means absolutely nothing. Many churches do not think in terms of membership (names on a list) at all, but in terms of engagement (persons actively sharing in tangible elements of the common life).

---

jobs that require them to go to work on Sundays—do we value these people? A lot of folks are never going to walk into a churchy-looking building, except for a friend's wedding or Grandma's funeral. Do we value these people?

- The growth of ministries to children and youth. As of 2018, American children second grade and younger are now all ethnic minorities, one hundred percent minorities—even the white kids. The white population majority has ceased to exist among young children. Within ten years, all American school children will be minorities.[21] By the time I reach my eighties, as a white person I too will be part of an ethnic minority, along with each of my fellow Americans.

- The development of the church's digital interface with the public. Almost anywhere they wish to go, people under the age of sixty[22] choose to travel first by smart phone.

The increasing demographic divide between the people in our churches and the folks all around us in the community should signal to us that in most churches, business as usual is not a reasonable way forward. Ours is a profoundly multi world that requires intentionally multi churches, with capacities for connections and relationships among people groups and worldviews. I understand that some churches are called to a demographic niche. There is a wonderful tradition in America of thriving churches for first generation immigrants, for example. But many American first generation immigrant churches that grew in the 1970s and '80s—and are now in free-fall—teaches us that valence matters. Even churches that specialize for a season in a very homogenous population must become increasingly multivalent after their first twenty years or so. Otherwise, they may find themselves in a place of dangerous disconnect from

---

21. D'Vera Cohn, "It's official: Minority babies are the majority among the nation's infants, but only just," Pew Research Center FactTank, June 23, 2016, http://www.pewresearch.org/fact-tank/2016/06/23/its-official-minority-babies-are-the-majority-among-the-nations-infants-but-only-just/.

22. Everyone under sixty in the year 2019 means everyone under seventy by the year 2029. As of this writing we are about two decades from the moment when many of the remaining tall steeple (and nonadaptive) churches will be reduced to small gatherings of octogenarians.

their children and grandchildren, not to mention all the neighbors who live around them.

All across North America, I can show you churches that were at the peak of institutional strength in the 1980s, and today they have collapsed. Take a tour of Orange County, California, for example, and drive in any direction. About every two minutes you will pass a church facility where ministry was thriving three decades ago—and where today the campus is very, very quiet. Some of these congregations were recently among the fastest growing in their denominational tribes. No more! These churches became as inert as neon gas, now focused mostly on life within the fellowship hall, populated by the aging faces in the church pictorial directory. Closed shells. How did this happen? Their valence might have been one or two in the best of years (meaning that they related well to one or two generations of church-going culture within one ethnic group), but now their valence has dropped to zero. These churches, often trapped in tired buildings that they can no longer afford to renovate, are now invisible to their neighbors, and mostly irrelevant.

As my sister once said when my brother-in-law dropped a hundred dollar bill on a roulette table in Vegas, only to see it scooped into a little slot by the dealer in a millisecond; "That was fast."

And indeed, it was fast—dizzyingly fast—the change in fortunes among the mostly white, suburban, denominationally affiliated churches in the United States, some of which were teaching us best practices just a few years back! But it's not just the white churches. The black congregations in my home city of Washington, D.C., are scrambling to figure out what a thriving ministry looks like in a city with a slowly diminishing black population and a decreasing level of participation among younger adults. Several Korean churches in northern New Jersey are in the same boat. And though many American Latinx churches are growing at the moment, this too will not last forever. The life conditions that are currently working to grow their current churches will change and challenge their future.

It is more than simply the ethnic shifts; the shifts in worldview among new generations in a post-Christendom culture are every bit as challenging. Put it all together, and one of the biggest changes that many churches have seen is the near disappearance of younger adults with children within the fellowship. And once a congregation loses a minimum critical mass of children and youth, they cease to offer a credible option to families of any ethnicity or worldview who might be looking for a place to raise their kids as people of faith. Ethnic change. Worldview change. Collapse of children's ministry. Ba-boom, a trifecta! And it was, indeed, fast.

However, any church can choose to shift toward a more multi type of vision. When churches do this, they may change the predictable narrative pretty quickly and discover a hope-filled future.

As churches awaken to a renewed sense of call to serve and partner with their neighbors, and to design ministry for and with their neighbors, multivalence is essential. When a church gets serious about offering different ways of connecting, styles of liturgy, ministry locations, times of gathering, mission projects and big ideas, the chances of a newcomer finding a relevant point of connection in that church go up! The fresh iterations of Christian community in such a church may not draw as many participants as in the past, but that church's future may be very bright nonetheless.

QUICK CHECK—WHAT IS THE VALENCE OF YOUR CHURCH?

(Answer "Yes" or "No" to each question. It is recommended that a group complete this, and that a list of participants be at the table, for spot-checking assumptions.)

1. Did more than 30 percent of your church's active participants grow up outside the Christian faith?
2. Does your church partner with any non-Christian faith group or congregation on a regular basis for worship, community service, or interfaith dialogue?
3. Are more than 10 percent of your church's active participants also working a twelve-step program or other recovery process?
4. Does your church offer at least two distinct styles of worship gathering each week with at least 20 percent of the total crowd in the smaller gathering?
5. Do more than 20 percent of your weekly worshipers attend church events on a day other than Sunday?
6. Is it acceptable for a person to bond with a particular group or ministry team without any expectation that she/he will join the church, attend worship, or pledge money? Or, more specifically, can we easily think of scores of persons who fall into this category—friends of our church, who choose to partner with us on their terms?
7. Are there at least two ethnic groups in your church that comprise more than 20 percent of your church's active participants? (The majority group counts as one.)
8. Does your church lack any ethnic majority on your lead team or on the stage on Sunday?
9. Are at least 40 percent of your church's weekly participants under the age of forty? Or are at least 25 percent of your church's weekly participants under the age of eighteen? (Choose only one of these questions.)

10. Does your church worship in more than one physical location?
11. Does your church worship in three or more physical locations?
12. Of the small groups and/or teams that function within your church's life (at physical locations or online), are at least 20 percent of them new in the last twelve months?
13. Do more persons engage your church online each week than show up in the building for major services and gatherings?

Add one valence point for each "Yes" that you could honestly answer. A score of 0–2 is normal for most churches—and probably inadequate for the years ahead. Totals of 3–5 indicate emerging multivalence—greatly enhancing your church's possibilities for the years ahead. (And for small congregations—excellent!) Greater than 6 means a multivalent church. Greater than 8: I would love to hear from you—and specifically to hear how (or if) you are managing to hold it all together without it blowing up!

Maybe the more important question for your church is where you would like to work to increase your church's bonding capacities with the people all around you! The church with a current valence of 3 can, in many cases, be at 5 within a couple years, if ministry development was focused in certain directions.

Wherever it is that you would like to go, and in whatever way you would like to stretch toward multivalence, you will find practical insights and tools in the pages ahead!

2

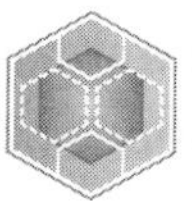

THE PRACTICES

It takes work to bond diverse people together into a church—and not just a one-time effort. Churches that originally developed within a homogenous culture may not realize the level of intentionality that is necessary for them to thrive as multi churches. Churches accustomed to a valence of zero or one don't have to work very hard to retain their very low state of energy. By work, I am referring to specific actions a church can take: activities, rituals, habits of life that will help to create the glue that holds diverse people together in a bond that is stronger than the forces at work to pull that church apart. The higher the valence that a church seeks to manage, the more critical such practices become!

In one sense, a compelling, common vision is often all the glue a church needs in order to hold together across considerable diversity of life experience and perspectives. That sounds simple enough—but the wider the range of people, the less simple it is. Discerning a vision that transcends the varied life experiences and concerns in a diverse church and that honors these multiple perspectives—that rarely happens casually. And retaining or renewing such a common vision also requires effort.

As one example of this: Edenton Street Church in Raleigh, North Carolina, has a high valence, with ministries that span multiple grids of human diversity. One of the big ideas that binds this church together across multiple locations is that *they exist to repair breaches in human community*.[23] Each of their Tables (the Edenton Street term for worship communities) focuses on healing different kinds of breaches.[24] For one Table, it is the breach between the Christian straight community and LGBTQ people. For another Table, it is the breach between black and white folks. For another Table, it is the political breach between red and blue political perspectives. For yet another Table, it is the breach between socioeconomic groups.

Recall the Florida church where I helped to plant two campuses. In the years after the three co-pastors had each left for other ministry opportunities, the relationship between the new pastors became more challenged. As a result, one of the campuses would split in two, and another would vote to become a

23. "Repairing the breach" is a term that MLK Jr. used in his sermon "The Drum Major for Justice," given February 4, 1968, at Ebenezer Baptist Church in Atlanta, Georgia.

24. Technically, Edenton Street's Tables represent four distinct churches organizationally, who voluntarily bind themselves in a common covenant around an overarching vision. This somewhat unusual internal organizational arrangement for a multisite church serves to preserve an appropriate level of self-determination at each Table.

freestanding congregation some eighteen years after it launched. As you might guess, there was considerable stress attached to these changes in that church's life. The glue of common vision that had effectively held that church together at one point ceased to hold after significant leadership turnover.

What is working well one year could cease to work well five years later. This is why certain practices, habits of life, are so critical. Any church that wants to juggle complexity of a multi ministry best not think that it gets easier over time—it does not. If a church becomes lax in any of the critical practices that we will look at in this chapter, their glue could begin to dissolve and their valence begin to fall—or rogue electrons[25] could begin to sabotage the church's unity. It is also possible that the maturing of a new ministry or circle of community within the larger church could take it to the place where it is simply time to "leave the nest" and continue growing beyond the connections in which it incubated. That should not be considered a failing!

There are critical practices that help to solidify relationship between leaders and to help them coalesce around common vision. These practices break into three broad themes: (1) prayer, (2) deep listening, and (3) clarifying identity and core commitments, offering coherence to the church.[26]

---

25. By "rogue electrons," I mean leaders who are not actively working toward holding the church together.

26. After I listed these, I realized that they corresponded roughly to the four areas of measure in the Readiness 360 process—spiritual intensity (prayer), dynamic relationships and cultural openness (deep listening), and missional alignment (coherence). "Readiness 360" is a very practical tool for any church that wants to move in a more multi direction. The report will not only share where the church currently stands in terms of its readiness for multi, but it also will offer leader tips in terms of practices to increase that readiness. See more at www.readiness360.org.

PRAYER

The church is God's thing, first of all, not our thing—a God-movement of love and human redemption stretching across the centuries. In our best moments, the church simply shows up to what God is doing. I have often said (about church planting) that we show up with a Bible, a broom, and a dustpan to assist in what God is already up to in a place. The Acts of the Apostles should more appropriately be named the Acts of the Holy Spirit. The very best apostles wouldn't have pulled off much of anything we read about in Acts had the Spirit of God not been driving the narrative.

The first-century church was arguably the most multi thing the world had ever seen up until that time: bridging barriers of economic class, ethnicity, language, gender, and nationality. It was very much a God thing, rooted in people's experience of Jesus and of Pentecost.

Multi is how God does.

Multi is what God does.

We may wish to do multi, but, apart from God, we often just make a mess. And so prayer is foundational, specifically prayer that focuses on (1) observing and claiming God's presence with us and (2) discerning God's will for us.[27]

Too often, prayer is associated with noise: incessant talking on our part, the long list of health concerns for our great aunts shared in small church gatherings, the wordy litanies that we say together. Granted, God invites us to ramble on in words, out loud together or in journal form, and endlessly. Jesus taught us

---

27. See Beth Estock, *Holy Living Series: Discernment: Spiritual Practices for Building a Life of Faith* (Nashville: Abingdon Press, 2019).

to pray with words—this is something that God sincerely welcomes. And yet, the best part of our praying often comes when the words run out, or just run dry.

Contemplative prayer is the space beyond the wordiness—where centering, and, often, better listening, occurs. It can happen through meditation on an image, a biblical word, or a memory. It may focus upon nothing more or less than our breathing. Elijah sitting in a cave, hearing the gentle whisper of the wind (translated "the still small voice" or "the sound of sheer silence"[28])—this image often comes to my mind as I think about contemplative prayer. After Elijah had exhausted his ego-stuff in righteous indignation before God, ranting and getting all his frustration out, things got quiet. And in the quiet, he finally heard God.

On a recent morning, three of us at the Epicenter Group[29] (Beth Estock, Trey Hall, and I) spent time reflecting on the relationship between contemplative prayer and Christian ministry in a multi age. Some of the jewels from that conversation follow:

- Given the amount of change and polarization going on in culture, we all find ourselves motivated by fear most of the time: fear of something. Fill in the blank.[30]
- Spiritual leaders must grow deep roots into something other than ego, fear, and the noise of daily life in order to be truly helpful and hopeful.

---

28. Phrase is taken from1 Kings 19:12, translated first in the Revised Standard Version and then in the New Revised Standard Version.
29. The Epicenter Group is my ministry coaching and consulting group, www .epicentergroup.org.
30. Of the seven shifts recommended in *Weird Church*, when I ask pastors where they need help, invariably most talk about the shift from fear to freedom.

- Whenever we operate primarily from a sense of should, ought, and must, we are not working from the Spirit.
- It is easy for spiritual leaders to find themselves at the end of their gifts and personality—working so hard and so well, and still it is not enough! Contemplation can be a way to stop working, just showing up to God.
- Contemplative leaders, to the degree that they are released from the tyranny of ego, are able to see beyond "us and them"—and so to lead their communities to resist othering[31] the people beyond the immediate fellowship.
- "Us and them" is an ethnocentric framework that is simply not workable for the twenty-first century. Given our current technology, it raises the risk of us destroying each other, and the planet as well. Our work is to help grow people's capacities for empathy and compassion.
- Yet this same framework functions differently across diverse communities. While breaking down "us and them" may be constructive for those communities that have historically operated with excess social and political power (especially white communities), it may present an entirely different challenge for communities that have historically operated in a context of oppression or marginalization. Communities' journeys into multi may vary substantially.

---

31. *Othering* is a term for how communities find security by identifying themselves as other than (fill-in-the-blank) people, and then distancing themselves from the "not us" people. It is easy to build communities as bastions of opposition to certain kinds of people, as a part of the community's most basic self-understanding. Of course, Jesus railed against this continually.

- People have always longed for a taste of the infinite—the ancient, the silence, the rituals—but increasingly these things have a hold on the hearts of postmodern people.

In all contemplative praying, we step into God-space. That is immensely helpful for all of us as we seek to find our spiritual bearings in a troubled and divisive age. But to create multi community, such prayer is more than helpful. It is essential.

Co-mingling contemplative prayer with scripture is a very old practice, reaching back to the early centuries of Christianity. Too often in modern Bible study, we lean hard into our left brains so that the whole study becomes abstract—talking about God rather than directly encountering God. As Bible reader(s) we keep a passive distance from the text. We step into the role of student more than spiritual pilgrim. There is great value in understanding the history, the characters, the famous interpretations—but, in the end, we are not studying for the LSAT. In our left-brain mode, we debate, dissent, and spar with ideas. Shifting to a less critical approach can open us up to practice our faith more inclusively. Lectio Divina[32] is probably the most popular method for doing contemplative Bible study. It focuses us away from the distractions of doctrine and critical method toward the simple encounter between our souls and the text. With a Lectio Divina approach, all kinds of folks can play together with scripture. People with sixth-grade education can engage with people who have PhDs. People whose political instincts lean in one direction can engage (more easily) with those whose instincts lead another way.

32. For a good summary of Lectio Divina, see www.contemplativeoutreach.org/category/category/lectio-divina.

I learned this firsthand more than a decade ago, working with a group of Latinx lay pastors, none of whom had college education. Though they had none of the advantages of biblical study that had been afforded me in three different academic settings from college to seminary to doctoral study, Lectio Divina enabled them to shine—and to work on the basis of how the text impacted their hearts—they were able to teach me as much as or more than I could teach them.

The challenge is to create a neutral space, side-stepping the tired human dividing lines of education, political alignments, ethnicity, immigration status, and so on. In such a holy space, when we encounter God together, we can transcend polarities. Ah-ha moments can occur. Transformation can unfold, for all of us!

DEEP LISTENING

Recently, at a delicious dinner party, a friend shared with our table how he decided to try hot yoga and almost had heatstroke —and, as scary as it sounds, the way he told it, we are all still laughing. It was a priceless story, revealing his humanity in a fresh way. A great evening is defined by breaking bread and sharing story—and it is no random accident that Christian worship is designed around those two poles of action.

A few days after the hot yoga story, I found myself in a California hotel while my internal body clock was still on East Coast time. So, at 5 AM, I was in the lobby, seated by the fireplace with my newspaper, waiting for a hotel worker to bring out the morning pot of coffee. By the time the coffee arrived, half a dozen of us were loitering like vultures. Small talk around the coffee gave way to conversation about jet lag, which led three people to volunteer that they had lived in or near D.C. (where I live). One woman, obviously the extrovert, stayed back and we chatted at length. She and her boyfriend live just five miles away from the hotel but wanted a weekend getaway on San Francisco Bay. I folded my newspaper. She and I began to share stories back and forth. She was born in the South Sudan. I was born in Austin, Texas. She has lived in the United States for thirty years. I have lived here my whole life. She faced the challenges of a new language and culture, yet she spoke like a lifetime Californian! I have read about Sudan, and seen documentaries, but she brought something abstract to life. Her story was so terribly rich, as was her hopefulness. I left the conversation blessed by the human connection—and by a fresh perspective on so many things. We are enriched when we hear stories and life reflections from persons whose experience differs from ours.

The sharing of stories weaves us together. It is a big part of how we become church to one another.

Several of the pastors that I work with have added storytelling components to their worship gatherings, in each case with positive response. One church invites an ordinary person to share a story relating to their life and personal faith in every gathering. In another, there are at least two stories shared, in addition to a biblical story, sometimes with a Lectio Divina type of process applied even to the nonbiblical stories. In another, an artist reflects on a piece of art and how it intersects with their life experience. Another community has experimented with slam poetry, a type of performance poetry that often asks hard questions of daily life and social authority. In yet another, the scripture is read by persons who are gifted enough to do live radio—so that humor and other subtleties come out in reading a particular passage. Even in gatherings so simple that the organizers might not call them worship, a group can spend time in a circle, asking each person to tell a personal story—whatever they wish to share—with time for the group to reflect and to offer blessing after each story.

In all cases, certain protocols should be observed around storytelling.

- **Respect.** I confess that in my exuberance, I am sometimes prone to interact in distracting ways. Good listening requires good manners. Whether in one-on-one conversation or in a group setting, honoring the storyteller is important. Equally important is pausing after the story is told in order to allow its words to sink in. Then after a moment of sitting quietly with the story, words of response can be shared.
- **Humility.** In the storyteller and in the listener(s), there must be an expectancy that everyone learns, everyone is enriched, everyone shifts, and everyone sees life in a slightly different light than before.
- **Authenticity.** This is one of the most prized aspects of faith-sharing in the twenty-first century—wherever and in whomever it can be found. So much religion feels plastic and soulless, to the point that a lot of people associate religion in general with fakery. There is a perception among many in the nonreligious population that people of faith are unwilling to veer off the official script and really engage in conversation. Authenticity is about showing people who we are and what we feel deeply, without pretense.[33]

---

33. Authenticity can also be faked and disingenuous. This dark art, seen in both the politicians and the religious, might fool some; but when people catch on to it, it becomes the death of any enduring credibility.

- **Trust.** Perhaps trust is the by-product of the above three capacities—but without trust, very little community ever forms.

Encounter and personal sharing, in the spirit just mentioned, can be programmed—but it is more powerful when it arises organically in our relationships out and about. After my dad died, I got ahold of his little red-leather King James Gideon New Testament. I read a good portion of it and came to the words of Paul in 2 Corinthians 1:12, as Paul thought back on his life and witness across the Roman Empire. He said, "We have had our conversation in the world." I really love that metaphor, even if it is not the most accurate translation of the original text: to think of our lives, and especially our lives in ministry, as a conversation. Life, at its very core, a conversation! A good news conversation! I am constantly coaching pastors and church planters to find their way into such conversation—not just with church folks, but with the wider array of human beings who live in their neighborhoods.

The business world often runs ahead of the church in the field of community listening. John Stoddard is an expert in Human-centered Design Thinking. He lives in Silicon Valley, formerly worked for IDEO, and now works with a Chinese start-up company, overseeing the design of their customer interface. Stoddard summarizes design thinking as having three core components: (1) human understanding and empathy, (2) organizational mission, and (3) technology.[34] Without item number one, the other two are basically useless.

---

34. John Stoddard, lecture given at Pacific School of Religion, February 24, 2018.

Stoddard's three components apply seamlessly to the design of Christian ministry. Churches have been challenged in all three areas in recent decades—in community relations, in alignment to the core mandates of Jesus, and don't get me started on how most churches lag behind embracing the digital culture! In design thinking, demographic analysis is not enough; you have to test the conclusions of that analysis in real conversation with live human beings. Design thinking shifts away from always viewing everything from the company perspective and starts looking at things through the eyes of prospective customers. This shift gives rise to an empathic way of viewing challenges—and often reframes the very nature of the challenge. A church planter who starts with a mission of creating a church for unchurched people in Oak Grove shifts her perspective to wonder: How can we (the church) help life to flourish in Oak Grove? Or how can we partner with the folks in whom the Spirit is already working in Oak Grove to invite the neighborhood into God's story? Can you sense how such a shift seems more God-oriented and less about church as institution or franchise?

Seek first the realm of God, and you will be surprised how often a functional, life-giving, sustainable local church will be added unto you!

Too often, the implicit mission of most churches is to create or to preserve a financially self-sustaining enterprise that can fund weekly worship services and the upkeep of funky buildings. When we get out into the neighborhood and immerse ourselves in the stories, a greater sustainability question emerges: "How can we contribute to a more sustainable life for the neighborhood, and for community writ large?" In other words, what's in it for the neighbors? The churches that can answer that question well may soon find themselves outgrowing their space. They will likely also discover pathways of financial sustainability.

But churches that don't get out of the fellowship hall echo chamber to engage their neighbors and to listen to their stories will soon cease to exist. Without engaged community listening, the church in America will exist largely as a hobby for a marginalized and eccentric 3 percent of the population.

CLARITY AND COHERENCE

I don't know who said it originally, but diversity is not an organizing principle. It is a community value, and sometimes a component of community-building strategy, but communities do not typically rally around their differences as the main attraction. Some churches that have achieved a reasonable amount of multivalence seem to forget this. It is easy for them to make the mistake of thinking that their diversity is the point and the draw.

Communities exist because of our commonality—which may be experienced amid our differences. This commonality is most often expressed in a common vision of life and in concrete values lived out in such a vision. Paul's most famous utterance on multivalence might be Galatians 3:28: "There is no longer Jew or Greek, there is no longer slave or free, there is no longer male and female; for all of you are one in Christ Jesus." The key words there are the last three: in Christ Jesus. That is the organizing glue. It is because of the "in Christ Jesus" that any of the rest of the statement is true. Without Christ, we are still siloed in all the aforementioned dimensions.

Every church needs something to hold tightly so that they can play loosely in another sphere. There has to be a set of common practices and culture that connects the circles of community and affinity as one body. In some cases, there is considerable uniformity of ministry design from one ministry group or worship community to the next. This sense of commonality makes it easier to grow a large network and avoid chaos that would undermine the mission.

The church that is very flexible theologically may be quite traditional liturgically or with respect to its decision-making. A church that is highly defined theologically may be more willing to innovate with worship and organizational forms. In all cases, some sort of coherence has to function as the glue. There must be something for all to hold tightly, and to hold in common. When it lacks a fresh sense of mission, birthed in Spirit encounter, a church is more likely to cling to whatever else it can find: be that thing the current arrangement of the chancel furniture or its perception of traditions.

When a church decides to expand its multivalence for any reason other than its understanding of God's call and its mission, there will be trouble. Sustainability is important, but it is not, of itself, a reason to go multi. Impressing the bishop by responding affirmatively to her challenge to become multi-whatever will do nothing to create the DNA needed for the challenge. Sustainability is essential. Bishops and other ecclesial managers can challenge us in holy ways, but if we respond to such issues without a true sense of the spiritual why, carried deep in our bellies, we will just spend a lot of money, make some people mad, sit in too many meetings, and burn out. Our efforts will feel institutional rather than organic.

Multi is the flavor of this century—not the flavor of the month, but of this era in human history. And it is the flavor of many churches that will thrive in the years ahead. So multi is becoming the sexy thing, and it will be easy to get caught up in the hype. But the hype cannot shape a common conviction about God's calling to your congregation. So a season spent in discernment may be the best next step! I sometimes tell churches, "Do your why work first, and then expand your ministry." Without a strong sense of *why*, churches are seldom compelling and magnetic. More than once, I have challenged a church to a season of discernment, digging deep within their collective heart to tap their driving *why*. Sometimes, the church's leaders just refuse to do it. When this happens, they sabotage any effort to develop a renewed ministry that feels relevant and compelling to their neighbors.

It is likely time at your church for a refresher on the question of "Why church?" if any of the following statements are true:

- Your church's mission is a rambling paragraph on the front of the worship bulletin that no one can remember, or which fails to capture the heart.
- Your church has operated with the same mission and values statements for more than a decade.[35]
- It is hard for your people to imagine any other way of doing anything you do than the ways you have been doing for the past few years.
- People under the age of fifty are disappearing from church life.
- Your church identity is mostly denominational and/or you use the denominational logo as your major brand graphic.

---

35. These may not need significant revision but simply significant revisiting. It is best to set the previous mission/vision/values documents aside to begin a fresh conversation. You can circle back to them after your process.

- The majority of the people in the church have been participants for more than a decade.
- The church has been shrinking steadily over multiple years.
- Leaders in the church think renewal can happen simply by adapting some best practices from another church, without wrestling in prayer.
- There is a renaissance of cultural or economic energy of some sort in the geographic neighborhood that is disconnected to what is happening inside the church.
- The church took the Readiness 360 survey and the composite index in the report came in under 310.

There are lots of great methods for doing vision/values/mission work. Whatever method you use or whatever ways you delineate mission and vision (and all that), I have some strong suggestions.

- Start with prayer. Spend a season rereading the Book of Acts or one of the Gospels, and pray. Practice contemplative prayer in your common life. This is often a very hard request for churches that have little experience in this kind of work. So get a facilitator if you need one. But don't jump into planning and research mode without doing some spiritual work. A major goal in starting with prayer is to let go of as many assumptions about your future as you can and open up to what God wants to show you.
- Get out into the community for deep listening. Some good resources for this work can be found on the Epicenter Group's website: www.epicentergroup.org. Talk to at least sixty people—if twelve people agree to talk to five each,

you are there. Let folks tell their stories. Take notes. Compare notes. Identify themes. This is also a time for researching community data—but always corroborate the data with the neighbors' and the community leaders' perceptions, and get their take on what it means.

- Pray some more. Write down every crazy idea that you can in response to what you are seeing and hearing. Reframe the question. You are not saving a church—you are called to something more. What is that something? Note the themes that emerge from all the crazy ideas. Pray some more.
- When the "ah-ha's" begin to emerge, hold them in prayer—and find consensus to act quickly and cheaply to test any ministry idea before remodeling the building or committing thousands of dollars and years of time!
- Collaborate with the neighbors on anything that you can do together that is legal and life-giving—and invite them to reflect with you on what was good in the experience. Share stories. Listen deeply.
- Pray some more.

Your church is not going to find its calling by isolating itself in contemplation on one hand, or by running around interviewing people on the other, without a sense of *why* you exist. After you have moved through the preceding steps, the church will be able to re-articulate its identity and calling in an afternoon, without the need to wordsmith things to death.

And then you will be much more ready for the multi journey that God has in store for your unique church!

3

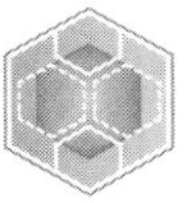

THE CAPACITIES — MULTICULTURAL

Chapters 3, 4, and 5 examine varied capacities of multivalence. Depending on which ones a church majors in and how it lives into those capacities, the ministry possibilities are endless! Some churches are hyperfocused on a certain capacity—for example, there is great interest these days in how to do multisite well and how to do multiethnic church with integrity. Those churches may be tempted to skip to the section of particular interest. Normally, I encourage such skipping around between chapters—but in this case, I suspect the most helpful section might be the one a church is most apt to skip. I encourage you to read and think about each of the capacities that we explore.

Some of the capacities overlap a bit—they certainly speak to one another. In all, these three chapters examine eight capacities, as follows:

MULTICULTURAL CAPACITIES (THIS CHAPTER)

- Multilingual
- Multinarrative
- Multiethnic
- Multigenerational

MULTIFAITH CAPACITIES (CHAPTER 4)

- Multitheological
- Multiliturgical

MULTILOCATIONAL CAPACITIES (CHAPTER 5)

- Multisite (physical meeting venues)
- Digital gathering

MULTILINGUAL

I have worked as a coach for two churches that intentionally interacted in both English and Spanish from their origin. In each case, considerable care was given to communication—and taking the time so that everyone was in the know on the most important things. In this way, all could access the teaching and also operate on an equal playing field in terms of church life and decision-making. A church can offer worship services in any number of languages, but if the major business of the church is conducted mostly in words that a significant constituency does not know, power becomes unequally distributed in the community.

In many bilingual American churches, most of the people in the non-English groups and worship services are bilingual. They worship in their heart language, but all week long they work and study in English—and they are able understand most of what is going on in their church. However, for those who are not bilingual, isolation can set in, and all sorts of misunderstandings. So, if your church has two or more language groups, it is a good thing to mix the people across language lines on a regular basis—with a translator in the room—so that we can all share a common experience and really get to know each other across the language barrier.

Power can also be distributed unequally around insider knowledge, even when everyone in the room operates in the same official language. In this case, the language barrier is not simply a matter of translation between Spanish and English (for example), but between people with long histories of thinking and talking about life with reference to certain theological or cultural traditions alongside those who are uninitated to such.

Have you ever walked into a room where people were speaking your formal language, but you still could not make much sense of what they were talking about? It happened to me most memorably when I took a seminar in American philosophy in college. I had not taken enough prerequisite courses in order to unlock the definitions and assumptions that came attached to the names and words that folks threw around that seminar table.

The course was all in English, my native tongue, but it could just as well have been in Swahili—most of it made no sense to me.[36] I recall one student kept saying, "it's *a priori*" (meaning *assumed from the start*), but I did not know the term and was

36. I made an A in that class, and I still didn't know half of what had been said—leading me to wonder if the course had been more an exercise in linguistic games and word intimidation than in understanding.

embarrassed to ask. I tried to look it up, but I did not know how to spell it. (It sounded like opry-something, as in Grand Ole'.) I finally ran across the term in a book a year later and I finally figured out what that guy kept going on about. This is the feeling a lot of people have walking into churches when they have not been initiated into the language.

All historic religions are loaded with terms and stories that have long history, by which insiders make sense of the world. If you are not schooled in a particular religion's backstory, going to church—or synagogue—or mosque—can be awkward, boring, embarrassing, frustrating, or all of the above. And let's face it. Christianity is not most people's first language for thinking about their lives, their big decisions, and the world about them. And, within the Christian world, a working knowledge of the vocabulary in use at the Episcopal Church may not be enough to help you at the Pentecostal Church.

Christianity is (like each of the great world religions) also very particular. Unique in many ways! We could talk about the particularity of the Christian concept of God as Trinity, but most Christians do not build their lives significantly upon abstract ideas. The way that Christianity attaches itself to our minds, habits, and decisions is more often related to the biblical stories, and of course, the overarching metastory of God's acts across history. Holy stories form the meat of faith as a life-language.

There are quite a few of us around who logged a lot of time early in life either at church or listening to Bible stories. We are a minority, and a shrinking minority, even at church! As biblical literacy has declined in American culture, so has the ability to think and act with reference to biblical stories, ideas, and principles.

On the bright side of this situation: acquiring Christianity as a second language is no longer a challenge only for nonchurch people. It is a challenge for most people, both within the church and beyond it. Two spiritual curricula are *not* required (one for the insiders and one for the outsiders). I take that as good news, at least in terms of simplifying our ministry challenge. Helping people acquire Christian faith as a formative and helpful life language is what we do, across the board.

Of course, in order to teach a language, we will need to be somewhat conversant in the various languages of the cultures we are seeking to engage. And it's an absolute Babel[37] out there. And, often, in here![38]

Several years ago, I attended this beautiful worship service on the Sunday after Epiphany, at a church where I was consulting. The whole service was about Epiphany: the origin of it, the meaning of it, and so forth. It was enjoyable enough until this thought went through my head: "What would the neighbors think of this service?" The service was a well-meaning attempt to teach late European Christianity as language to those gathered. But it was a little like the first day of French class in ninth grade, when our teacher rode a bicycle into the classroom speaking French to us and refused to engage us in English for the entire hour. I had signed up for French, but I was at a loss until the teacher finally started speaking a little English. On the other hand, the public (churched and unchurched) that we are seeking

37. See Genesis 9, where Babel symbolizes the chaos and lack of common understanding that often breaks our pride in how much progress we are making as a society.

38. How often have we witnessed breakdown in common understanding within the church fellowship as profound as any breakdown in the wider society?

to engage is not forced to return week after week. And they grow quickly impatient with insider talk and concerns that do not touch them in the life-language that they currently speak.

We have to become multilingual to some extent in order to do the work of evangelism in our time. We are asking the public to become multilingual—to acquire the language of Christianity—so it's only reasonable that we should also be multilingual and seek to understand at least core ideas, values, and constructs of the cultural context in which we find ourselves. Spiral Dynamics[39] and Mosaic Groups[40] can be helpful to us here in making sense of the cultural language. But these simply represent book learning. For the church leader interested in really learning the languages in the neighborhood, you have to immerse yourself in the neighborhood, and get into conversation—especially conversation that is entirely without reference to the church.

Please remember that in a multilingual world:

- The church needs to say things simply and in terms that make sense to the widest public. We should continuously

---

39. To help you identify where your ministry context falls within the worldview options of Spiral Dynamics, I recommend *Weird Church: Welcome to the Twenty-First Century* (Cleveland: Pilgrim Press, 2016), which I wrote with Beth Estock.

40. When I draw up a community study using the tools offered by Mission Insite, the thing that I find most helpful is the breakdown of Mosaic Groups within the community. No two neighborhoods are exactly alike. There are seventy-one groups in the United States, developed by Experian as an exercise in consumer lifestyle segmentation. Mission Insite, partnering with Experian Marketing Services, has studied each of these seventy-one groups in terms of questions relevant to spirituality, social values, and religious affinity. To learn more about Mosaic Groups: experian.com/assets/marketing-services/product-sheets/mosaic-usa.pdf. To see how Mission Insite has developed deeper understandings of these groups: missioninsite.com/PDF_Files/Mosaic_Descriptions%20Group-Segments_%20USA%20Final%20Cover%20081312.pdf.

ask ourselves if something we wish to say or do would make any sense to a person who has little experience (or interest) with church or with the Bible. And even if it made sense, would it be deemed relevant to their life concerns?

- Consider inviting an expert in local culture onto the worship planning team, or someone who is extremely conversant with local ways and language. This person might be a spiritual seeker, a person new to your church's flavor of life, a person from a different ethnic background than the church majority or from a younger generation. I once found a volunteer for worship planning who was a walking encyclopedia of movies, music, and pop culture. Be sure this team member will speak up confidently when something makes no sense or seems odd in order to help find better ways forward in worship design.
- Languages, once acquired, have to be used. We must stay engaged in the language and life concerns of our neighborhood, engaged especially with people outside the walls of our church if we expect to become or to remain culturally fluent!
- It is unrealistic to expect one pastor to be fluent in every life-language in a diverse neighborhood. While that pastor needs to be out in the neighborhood, she also needs a multilingual team at the table where ministry design happens. Diversity at the ministry planning table is so essential—indeed, this theme echoes with each of the multi capacities.
- Interviews (both with people in the church and beyond it) are excellent tools for a multilingual ministry. These interviews can be live on stage in a worship gathering or they can be video-recorded and saved. Either way, this is an

excellent way of helping people make linguistic shifts between one way of framing and saying something, to another way. Start with a person's story in their vernacular and worldview, and then explore the theological implications that cast new light on their story, perhaps referencing stories with similar issues or dynamics in the biblical tradition.

- The two most common reasons for boring sermons, in my view, are (1) the preacher is bored and not growing personally, and (2) the preacher is making little effort to express God's good news in ways that take into account the language(s) of the neighborhood. My friend and former client, Adam Weber, is pastor of Embrace Church, a multisite church in South Dakota and Minnesota. Adam is highly fluent in the life-language of the people in his mission zone. Preaching that targeted the relevant concerns of young people in the upper Midwest was one of the most important factors contributing to the rapid growth of Embrace Church in its early years.[41] Down on the Gulf Coast, Pastor Sam Persons Parkes in Mary Esther, Florida, amazes me with his integration of southern life experience into his preaching, in ways that might not work up in the Dakotas. North of Los Angeles at Valencia United Methodist Church, Pastor Nicole Reilley provides another example of the artful integration of cultural fluency and gospel. These skilled preachers remind me that the gospel is both universal and profoundly local. If I were to walk into any of the

41. Embrace Church launched Sunday morning worship in 2009. As of 2017, it had gathered more than four thousand worshipers per weekend in two states in five physical locations and another two thousand per week online.

aformentioned churches, as a local resident, I would likely be surprised by both the wit and insider wisdom about local life experience.[42]

MULTINARRATIVE

Behind the many languages of the Babel around us, there are stories. Real life stories—not cartoons, not parables, not TV dramas! To know my language is to begin to discover how I see life and the world. And to know my story is to know why I see it that way—and to begin to know me as a unique child of God, and not just a (fill in the blank with my demographic).

The multinarrative capacity builds directly upon the storytelling practice lifted up in chapter 2. Some churches seek to embed a capacity for different kinds of life narratives within the heart of the community: trusting narratives and questioning narratives, celebration narratives and lament narratives.

In our polarized world, it is tempting to simplify our lives by barricading ourselves in closed-shell echo chambers (in our media choices, in our choice of friends, in our choice of church) where the stories that we tell are never challenged by another person's experience. These sorts of narrative gaps, and the consequent distrust that has taken hold in the political world, will not be easily changed anytime soon. In politics, so long as you have a majority of voters on your side, you can ignore the rest of the people. But in Christian ministry, God does not give us any such option. As servants of Christ, we have an obligation to the people in our neighborhood, to listen to them. They, however, have no obligation at all to listen to our side of things—we have to earn that

42. Visit maryestherumc.org and umcv.org.

right—by listening well and by demonstrating with action that we wish to be a part of solutions, and not just more of the problem(s).

When, in Luke 10, Jesus sent the seventy out two by two into the community, they had no particular program to establish, no curriculum or Bible lessons to teach. They had simply their stories and, more particularly, their humanity to share, one with the other. So when, occasionally, someone answered the door with twinkling eyes, and they offered shalom and food to the travelers who had come down their lane—magic happened. And the realm of God visited the house. Jesus warned the seventy missionaries not to bounce from house to house, but when they found welcome, to enter there, and sit down for a season.

My ideas as your neighbor may be off base from your sense of reality, but my experience is my experience. To know my story is to know, in truth, what life is like for me. To listen to my story makes whatever story you might have to share back all the more compelling—because deep listening earns the listener credibility in all times and places.

If you can think of any group of persons who would be unwelcome at your church sharing their stories in such a way, this should serve as a red flag. Those stories are perhaps the ones you are most in need of hearing. In order to hear such stories, it might be that our members need first to observe a fast from talk radio and cable channels that constantly demean persons of different life experiences and values.

Every so often, I lead seminars with church leaders where we invite local people outside the church to come in as a group of panelists so that they can tell their stories and talk about their perceptions and experience of churches. I have emceed groups of young adults as they shared their stories with a room full of boomers. I have emceed nonchurch people as they shared their stories with a room full of pastors. It is always an eye-opening conversation.

Deeply absorbing a neighbor's story is more than simply understanding how to position your message in the neighborhood. A compelling narrative gets into your subconscious and your dreams.[43] It is transformative at some level. Stories change us. Maybe that is why we sometimes resist listening to the people whose life experiences contradict our own narratives. Maybe that's why parents whose children turn out to be gay so often tend to change their own internal narrative about sexuality. Maybe that's why people who get to know undocumented[44] persons within their church fellowship as sisters and brothers and colleagues in ministry often come to view the U.S. immigration debate differently. Maybe that's why the soldiers on patrol in Jerusalem the year I was there (1998) worked in teams of two—one Israeli and one Palestinian. When your enemy is your partner, it does enhance the possibilities for peace in the city.

From the Day of Pentecost, the invitation into the adventure of Christian fellowship has offered an experience of never-ending opportunity for personal transformation through deep listening to multiple narratives. This kind of transformation is threatening to those who want to keep the world divided into "us and them," and to demonize certain populations. If our tribal ideology is

---

43. In Acts 10, even though Peter had already had a mind-bending dream, it was not until he met Cornelius and heard his story that Peter said, "I realize now how true it is that God does not show favoritism, but accepts from every nation the one who fears (God) and does what is right."

44. Persons who reside in the United States without documented status issued from the government.

more precious to us than the gospel, we will likely resist a multinarrative ministry.

How are faith communities developing a radical multinarrative approach?

- A long-established church in Colorado Springs offers worship gatherings twice a month called Stories @ the Edge. Pastor Tiffany Keith and her friends construct each gathering around different stories, told directly by those involved. One of the stories is often, by design, told from outside the faith assumptions of the majority gathered.[45] They move beyond an echo chamber in order to better appreciate their neighbors.
- A New York City church organized small groups with NYU students, and one of the students wanted to create a group in which he could try to recruit persons away from Christianity. They let him try. He later became a Christian, a thing that almost certainly would not have happened without the church's acceptance of his dare.[46]
- An evangelical Michigan church has a weeknight men's group that meets in a community pub, led by the pastor. The only rule for attending is that you have to come with serious doubts about some aspect of the Christian faith.[47] They read atheist authors, Christian authors, and others.

---

45. See www.theedgedowntown.org, a ministry of First United Methodist Church in Colorado Springs.

46. See leadershipedges.com.

47. Sycamore Creek Church in Lansing calls this the Agnostic Pub Group. According to pastor Tom Arthur, they call it agnostic because it is for people who find themselves somewhere in between atheist and believer.

- There is a worldwide movement born in Mexico and now hosting events in major cities all over the world. It is called F*ck Up Nights. No kidding. It is a gathering where young entrepreneurs encourage one another by sharing stories of their business failures. Often held in pubs, with lots of laughter, they curate one story after another in the genre of "Wylie Coyote, super genius!" The power of this gathering is that it frees people from the paralyzing fear of failure: to keep trying, to keep stretching, and to be okay with the rough and tumble of their journey toward innovation. It models for the church what authenticity looks like as they seek to encourage one another on the journey.[48]

In the world that is unfolding, we must be willing to listen well to the stories of our neighbors—especially to those stories that create a little tension, that challenge us to ask questions, in a setting freed from anyone's compulsion to sweep everything into a tidy resolution by the end of the evening. Many churches can't hear narratives from outside the majority point of view or experience without filtering or without resolving everything in an hour. What does that say about us? For most folks outside our circle, it would say that we have not yet convened a safe place for them to be who they are.

Storytelling and listening builds trust. And trust will help some folks to open up to the possibilities of a Christian narrative. But listening to multiple narratives is not primarily a recruiting device. It is a practice intended for the healing of the neighborhood (and our own healing in relationship to the neighborhood)!

---

48. See www.fuckupnights.com.

MULTIETHNIC

The multiethnic church[49] has been around in the United States for a good while, dating back at least to the birth of the Pentecostal movement in Los Angeles in 1906. Prior to 1906, multiethnic churches were rare in America.[50] More than a hundred years later, the Sunday worship hour is in many places still the most segregated hour of the week. But this is changing.

Churches with a Pentecostal/charismatic edge are more likely to embrace a multiethnic fellowship than other churches. But, in the last quarter century, we have seen a steady increase in multiethnic churches beyond the Pentecostal community, especially with populations that are more practiced in interethnic collaboration. In my Readiness 360 research, I identified three populations within the church membership that correlate with elevated cross-cultural capacities. These populations are young adults, people with urban life/work experience, and military persons. Living in an ethnically diverse neighborhood, working in ethnically egalitarian organizations, growing up with ethnically diverse friends and (especially) marrying across ethnic lines—each of these life experiences equips people with skills that are helpful in the development of multiethnic churches. My friend Sam Rodriquez, on the Religion and Race team of the United Methodist

---

49. Ethnicity is about people groups. To say a church is multiethnic is to say there are multiple people groups coming together as church. There are typically issues of both race and culture at play within an ethnic identity. Some cultures are racially mixed; some races are culturally mixed. I choose to use the term "multiethnic" here with the knowledge that issues of dominant race and dominant culture are involved.

50. Churches in the eighteenth and nineteenth centuries that forced persons of color into balcony seating were so segregated that they fell short of being multiethnic at the core of their identity.

Church, sums all of this up in a word: relationship.[51] As we become more skilled in relationship with persons of other ethnic backgrounds, we are able to go places in the development of our faith communities that our grandparents likely would not have been ready for.[52]

When I ask pastors of multiethnic churches if they believe that we are reaching a tipping point where the numbers of such churches are going to suddenly proliferate, their answers are tentative. They see growing multiethnic capacity in the church's future, but the future is always hard to read—and rarely arrives as fast as we might hope. Racism makes the pursuit of multiethnic ministry the trickiest type of multivalence, especially if white people are involved (or any group that has a history of abuse and inappropriate power waged against another group). As I write this, the United States, in particular, has entered an era of renewed reckoning around race and national identity. The time fast approaches when neither the United States nor Canada will have any racial majority. Conscious racist resentment is growing in North America, with public endorsement of white privilege coming from President Trump himself—portending what could be a tumultuous and painful road ahead. White Americans are being forced to share their historic social, economic, and political dominance with others. And, as the nation deals with this, we are still processing the racism that was woven into the country's origins, especially in terms of the institution of slavery and of the westward expansion that violently marginalized the Native American population.

---

51. Interview with Sam Rodriquez January 5, 2018.
52. See Cole Brown's excellent article, "3 Concerns About Pursuing Multi-Ethnic Churches," www.thegospelcoalition.org, Sept 13, 2017.

In the next two decades, the multiethnic church could be a game changer for our larger society. As more of us experience persons of other ethnic identities as our spiritual siblings, the Holy Spirit may help us achieve what our politicians have had difficulty delivering.

I know this much: the longing for a church that transcends racial segregation and white supremacy is growing faster than the visible reality of such a church. Just after the turn of the century, I led an exploration retreat in the southern United States for potential church planters and their spouses. Toward the end of each of fifteen interviews, I went off the script of prepared questions and just let these couples talk. Every one of them, unprompted, and without knowledge of the other fourteen conversations, confessed a deep longing to lead a church that was multiethnic. What were the odds of this? I took it as a God sign.

Toronto, Ontario, is one of the most multiethnic cities in the world, and the most racially diverse metropolitan area in Canada. And yet—as is true almost everywhere—most of Toronto's churches are rooted in a particular ethnic heritage. And they often retain that heritage even in a profoundly multiethnic city. There is some mixing, of course, but for the most part, the white churches stay mostly white. The Chinese churches stay mostly Chinese. The Caribbean churches stay mostly black.

Twenty years ago, Cornerstone Church was a new church of second-generation Chinese Canadians, many of whom had been raised in a vibrant center-city Toronto church where the primary language was Cantonese. For these emerging young adults, it was not enough that they develop an English language service—they longed for a church that reflected the full diversity of their city—and the diversity of the realm of God.

Andrew Lau, Cornerstone's founding pastor, became convinced that multiethnicity was God's plan for the church. For Andrew, this was more than a strategic issue to market the church as a diverse community. It was a theological issue, rooted in the very nature of God. The association of Chinese Baptist churches expressed great ambivalence about Andrew's vision for the new church. The original vision of the Chinese Baptists was to establish churches to reach Cantonese-speaking immigrants in southern Ontario. But twenty years later, Cornerstone has developed into a church without any ethnic majority on most Sundays among the seven hundred persons gathered in worship, even though the host culture is still Chinese Christian.

Multiethnic churches are sometimes defined as communities where the dominant ethnic group comprises less than 80 percent of total active participants. Although some churches emerge with no ethnic majority, most multiethnic churches will retain a majority of some sort. Andrew Lau terms this ethnic majority "the host culture." A host culture naturally brings outsized influence and assumptions to the table—and this can easily override the cultural wisdom and influence of other ethnic groups unless great care is given. At Cornerstone, biblical hospitality is the key to a host culture's healthy functioning in a multiethnic context.

When I asked Pastor Melissa Maher of Mercy Street Church in Houston how she would define host culture in her multiethnic congregation, I expected to hear something about southern Anglo culture (about 60 percent of Mercy Street's people). What I heard instead was recovery.[53] The experiences of recovery,

53. Conversation with Melissa Maher, January 24, 2018.

twelve-step journey, nightly meetings, and rehab form such a powerful sense of common culture that other aspects of multivalence are made easier. This is similar to what sometimes occurs in a robust Pentecostal situation—the primary host culture is a common (and intense) experience of the Holy Spirit. In multiethnic recovery churches and Pentecostal churches, the larger questions of host culture and hospitality may be more about how to make space for persons who have not experienced twelve-step community or been baptized in the Spirit. But the principle of host culture is still operative in most cases.

HOST CULTURE AND HOSPTALITY

A healthy host culture is one of the major foundations of a well-functioning multi church. To have a hospitable host culture, the following components should be present:

1. Humble awareness on the part of the people in the host culture that they continue to carry out-sized influence in the life of the church, based on the church's particular heritage and/or the experiences of a majority of the church's participant/members. This consciousness among the persons connected to the historic traditions and power within the church is essential in order to become a truly multi church.
2. A strong commitment to hospitality toward persons outside the host culture, based primarily upon the call of the gospel, not upon issues of institutional survival or other pragmatic considerations. The driving question: "How can we create an environment where a person who is not a part of our historic host culture can find a true sense of spiritual home here?"
3. Intentional empowerment of persons within the church who are outside the host culture, by making space for them at the decision

table, in worship leadership, and in other places at the heart of the church's life. In this way, key places at the heart of things function as the venues where the church lives into multi life. Church leaders work through the challenges together and on a smaller scale, even as they invite the larger community into a multi life.

4. Owning specific aspects of the host culture, which can be offered as a gift to those who come from beyond that culture. Examples: the recovery church that wishes to join persons who are not part of any twelve-step group into experiences and practices rooted in the wisdom of the twelve steps, the LGBTQ-majority church that wishes to invite straight people to think about the ways that all of us have to "come out" in life and faith, the Korean-heritage church that wishes to teach the practice of early morning prayer, or the black-heritage church that wishes to invite persons outside the black experience to discover the power of liberation theology as it may also apply to their lives.
5. Following the example of the first-century church, leader representatives of the host culture open themselves to the truth that God's future for the church always transcends the cultural heritage of any particular group. So they open themselves to collaboration with the Spirit and with those from other cultural experience as midwives of the church, which God is calling to life.

In churches with strong multiethnic valence, there may still be vital possibilities and need for racially homogenous small groups. Christian Washington, pastor of Upper Room Church in the Heights neighborhood of Houston, leads a congregation in which the largest racial group is black, but where there is now no clear ethnic majority on the part of any group. Even at Upper

Room, with persons of multiple races in worship leadership every Sunday, and a very high degree of ethnic interaction, the majority of their small groups still lean heavily toward a particular racial identity and experience. About a third of their groups could be said to be multiethnic,[54] meaning that two-thirds are not. This illustrates that a lot of folks will still need places of life affinity, especially in terms of common ethnic experience. Sometimes we all need to huddle with others who share very specific challenges of our life experience just to process our faith in light of our shared context. Don McGavran was correct on this point.

Churches that wish to increase their capacity for multiethnicity should consider the following strategies:

- Work with a church of a different ethnicity on a common ministry—a local mission endeavor or a common youth ministry—where folks can work as peers in ministry.
- Worship with a church of a different ethnic culture on a regular basis. Pentecost Sunday is an obvious option, but this can be done almost any season of the year—and do it on Sunday.
- Look for persons within the congregation who have a heightened capacity for leadership in a multiethnic space because of their own life experience (such as careers in industry, education, government, or the military). Convene them as a multiethnic prayer team to begin dreaming together of what might be possible.
- Invite young adults into conversation and prayer about a next-generation ministry development that pushes beyond

54. Interview with Christian Washington, January 5, 2018.

where the church has historically been. Young adult fellowships often need to be nurtured apart from the larger church for a season in order for them to develop as disciples and grow in number. This is even more essential when the ethnic mix of the young adult population is different from the church as a whole.

- Work first on another capacity of multi (beyond race), which is less challenged by a long and complex history of relationship between groups. Improving a church's capacity for nurturing a multinarrative community, for example, will make it easier to tackle race—because deep listening will be required!

Finally, we must note that the intersection between black and brown and white in America is fraught with accumulated centuries of complexity and pain. There is never a point where a church can relax fully and say "mission accomplished" with regard to the healthy integration between persons in groups of privilege and persons in groups that have experienced injustice. Issues of white privilege are so insidious and woven into the habits of the larger culture that churches must remain in a state of constant vigilance and repentance in order for there to be healthy relationship of leaders and of congregants across racial intersections. However, if the leader team[55] will stay attuned to this dynamic and talk about it regularly, the Spirit of Pentecost can enable the church to model what healing looks like for the larger society.

55. And especially the persons on the team who identify as white.

MULTIGENERATIONAL

When I was a child, I was part of a one-hundred-year-old county seat First Church with a good number of people in every age category. Many of the church's members had spent their entire lives in that one congregation. To find such a church today is not easy. In fact, multigenerational capacity within churches may be declining in North America, at least for a season.

The population of seniors in many long-established churches has remained steady and kept paying the bills, but adults under the age of sixty have all but vanished in many historic congregations.[56] Even in those outlier churches where a strong presence of young and middle-aged adults has persisted or reemerged, the younger folks typically make up a smaller portion of the overall congregation per capita than in years past. This is not a sustainable situation. Time is catching up with the churches that failed to retain multiple generations. Churches where funerals were rare two or three decades ago may now be facing such events almost weekly; many of those churches are now facing the final movement of church collapse as their donor base rapidly leaves this earth.

---

56. Even in renewing congregations, often we see an emergence of very young adults alongside seniors, and a missing gap of persons ages thirty-five to sixty (the highest income segment of the population). Paul Moon, one of our Epicenter Group associates, believes that the most critical cultural shift is between those persons who started with a computer in their twenties and those who did not. If you have lived in a digital world since your twenties, you are less likely to be active in the world of organized religion. Since the first personal computer appeared in 1981 and infiltrated offices and classrooms within a few short years, this means that if you were born after 1960, you probably integrated digital habits into your life from the time you graduated college or earlier, and you are less likely to be engaged in a mainline church than had you been born in 1950.

For every three adults under the age of sixty who have gone missing from First Presbyterian or All Saints Episcopal, roughly one of the three landed at a nondenominational church or other new church specifically designed for a generation restless with church-as-usual.[57] If it were not for these churches with ministries designed to catch folks on their way out the door, we would likely be looking at a collapse of organized religion in America more on the scale of what has occurred in western Canada, Australia, and much of Europe. (So kudos to all the church planters and ministry entrepreneurs in the United States who specialize in reaching younger generations!)

A close examination of the demographics of nondenominational churches (and of new congregations designed for the rising generation of adults) will show that most of their people were raised within one brand or another of American denominational Christianity. These upstart churches may feel a strong mission to design ministry in a way that reaches the "spiritually lost" people or the "unchurched." And, indeed, they do report some converts—but most of their people have history in church.

A couple decades back, denominational churches caught on to some of these trends and began to mimic the nondenominational churches in worship style in order to retain younger people. This adaptation enabled thousands of churches to remain multi-

57. This is based upon multiple Mission Insite population studies of parish areas all over the United States, as I have consulted with hundreds of congregations, using the Quadrennium Report tool. The Quad report accurately estimates religious activity and religious self-identification utilizing a variety of data inputs. The trends are remarkably consistent in almost all parts of the United States.

generational,[58] but at a cost. Attendance in traditional worship services often plummeted, leaving half empty sanctuaries, while all the younger folks were gathered in a different room or a different hour. A generation later, these 1990s worship innovations often feel more tired than the sanctuary services. People who stayed on with old First Church twenty years ago (because of the contemporary service) are now dismayed to see their adult children moving on.

However, based on research from the Barna organization,[59] I think we would be premature in giving up on the idea of multigenerational churches in our time. The thousands of millennial adults they interviewed gave evidence of several deep longings where churches have opportunity for renewed multigenerational relationship. Cooler music did not make the top five. Nor are they specifically asking for a preacher in flip-flops. They do, however, often long for mentors in their lives. They long for help finding their personal sense of purpose. The ministry must feel relevant to their lives. If there is a project at hand (at work or at church), they want to be treated as competent collaborators—they want to be full participants at the table.

I would supplement these conclusions with a few reminders.

- People who would consider participation in a church typically are looking to build relationships with other people

---

58. During my years as a director of church development for one of the UMC conferences, we placed a focus on churches starting as many new worship communities as possible. This was a major factor in that conference experiencing net gains in total numbers of people four out of five years 2002–07, during a time when few conferences posted any such gains.

59. Documented in Barna Group, *Making Space for Millennials: A Blueprint for Your Culture, Ministry, Leadership, and Facilities* (Ventura, CA: Barna Group, 2015).

their age and life-stage. This is as true for older adults as for younger adults.

- Vital children's ministry is essential, where people's kids can become engaged. When launching children's ministry, about twenty-five active grade-school children are minimum in order for community people to take it seriously.
- Culturally competent, relevant preaching by a person of similar age and stage is almost always a piece of the puzzle when we study why certain churches reach so many younger adults. So in terms of a multigenerational church—a multigenerational preaching team always makes sense.
- Convening a multigenerational team for the deep rethink is required to create fresh space for multigenerational faith community! (And the spiritual energy and motivation for the team must be deeply rooted in the younger folks.)
- Plan new ministry on a lean budget! When millennials and others without a lot of personal church experience do engage, we can expect their per capita financial contributions to be less than half of the monetary levels we came to expect from the folks who are dying off, and possibly less than one fourth! Lean ministry models and multiple funding streams are in order.

That multigenerational county seat church my father pastored fifty years ago has weathered the last half century reasonably well and is still roughly the same membership as back then. Just a few years back, I consulted with another congregation in the same town. During the Sunday school hour at the church where I was working, I headed down the street to old First Church. As I walked up to the neo-Gothic sanctuary at a few minutes before 11 AM, I heard what sounded like drums. I thought to myself, "No way, not here, not at 11 AM!" When I walked in, the place was about half full, with a wide variety of ages scattered about the room surrounded by the same glorious stained glass windows that I remembered from my youth. A youth band spread out across the chancel, leading in music. One old man recognized me and rolled his eyes with a grin about the changed worship style. When I reflected with my mother on how surprising this all was, she replied, "That church always valued young people." As a result, First Church made some critical choices, which to some may have felt like sacrifices. In the end, for these folks who had been nurtured in faith across multiple decades, their mission was to give their church away to the next generations of people. They held that value above the value of tradition, and, in so doing, they had retained the gift of a multigenerational church.

The church where I was consulting, on the other hand, had experienced some kind of internal blowup over worship style a decade earlier and most of their younger people had left en masse to join the nondenominational church on the edge of town. Wise church leaders will choose to let younger people take the lead. It is unfortunate that so many churches have failed to do so. Because when the young people are gone, in most cases, they are gone for good.

4

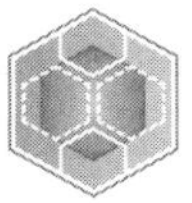

THE CAPACITIES — MULTIFAITH

Chapter 3's multi capacities each deal with issues of culture. Now we move into the terrain of how we practice faith. One might ask, "Why would any church wish to take their multivalence into the substance and content of their faith?" Would this not invite confusion of belief and theological relativism? Would this not risk watering down the core consensus around which demographic diversity can occur? In fact, even very conservative churches are often multivalent in terms of faith perspectives! The key (as in all matters of multivalence) is finding strong core agreements so that we can tolerate differences on other matters.

This chapter examines two particular kinds of multifaith capacity: the first is straightforward disagreement on various beliefs. The second flows from the first: when there is some range of belief diversity tolerated within a church, how does it impact worship and core activities in a church's common life? There is, in many places, a reverse correlation between these two: the more latitude that is tolerated theologically, the more tightly a church defines itself by its practices; the more consensus it demands theologically, the more freedom for innovation it has in practices.

MULTITHEOLOGICAL

Opening up space to disagree on some beliefs certainly could invite chaos, but applied artfully, churches have nothing to fear from creating a bit of defined bandwidth and variety in range of viewpoints. In fact, many churches already have a significant range of theological viewpoints and simply do not acknowledge the fact. A church that can tolerate a certain range of beliefs invites a wider audience of persons into participation and teaches persons how to model patience and dialogue in love with one another. In order for a multitheological approach to work, however, there should still be a common core of critical belief that does not vary much around the room—or, where it does vary, people understand the church's official positions. As discussed in chapter 2, there must be missional coherence among the church's leaders, and this coherence must be expressed theologically. Churches—and people in general—organize around that upon which we agree. An infinite range of theological viewpoints does not work within a single ministry or faith community, regardless of where it finds itself on any theological spectrum.

But, remember: ever higher valence is not the point anyway.

There is a difference between two persons being theologically different and them being theologically at odds with one another.

Almost everyone reading this can think of somebody in their experience who saw some things differently, but who made for great friends and ministry partners nonetheless. The reason such relationships work is because the persons involved discern and articulate enough common ground that they can move past their differences. It is unwise to partner anybody (or any church) with another as ministry partners unless there is significant and compelling common ground between. Synergy presupposes common ground! Functional megachurches—and functional political parties—may invite rather diverse coalitions of folks together, but always on the basis of common values that are clearly identified and celebrated.

In Chapter 1 I spoke of the way that people are able to latch onto certain works of art for differing reasons. I have a friend who recently visited an art museum in Portland, Oregon. He saw a painting and posted it on Facebook. The meaning of the work was ambiguous, but he loved it. It connected to his story in specific ways that cannot be generalized to my own story. If I were to bond with the same piece of art, my point of connection would be different. Great art offers multiple points for connection.

As the biblical text is a form of art, the same could be said about the way we find meaning in scripture. Some texts are profoundly multivalent. This is why people of multiple generations and experiences can experience meaningful worship in the same room at the same time. The text hits us each differently! In the Hebrew Scriptures, persons from three major world religions find different meaning in common stories. Among Christians, we often cite the Gospel texts of Christ's passion, the parable of the Good Samaritan, or the twenty-third Psalm as scriptures that always inspire. My dad used to tell me to preach on such texts as often as possible, because you have to really work to pull a bad sermon from such great material! These passages offer seemingly endless ways for people to connect to them and to find meaning in them.

At times, someone may find little interest in the implications of a literal interpretation of a Bible story, yet the metaphors arising from the story can be deeply captivating, connecting with any number of life issues. Some points of deep meaning may even move beyond anything the original author of the text imagined.

The multivalence of scripture varies from church to church. Some churches with a highly defined set of beliefs may insist that only the church's official interpretation of any scripture be taught within any class or gathering. Other churches with a shorter list of essential beliefs allow latitude on scriptural interpretation, in the spirit of the admonition: "in essentials unity, in nonessentials, liberty, and in all things, charity."[60] Churches that tolerate a very wide range of theological and scriptural points of view invariably have some other organizing energy, such as commitment to high church liturgy and pageantry in worship or a profound commitment to issues of social justice.

Each church must articulate what, exactly, is essential. And each generation must review the consensus of their forebears.

---

60. These words are often attributed to John Wesley, probably by mistake. Church historian Richard Heitzenrader (chapter entitled, "'Unity, Liberty, Charity' in the Wesleyan Heritage," in the book *Unity, Liberty, Charity: Building Bridges under Icy Waters*, edited by Donald Messer and William Abraham (Nashville: Abingdon, 1996), states that these words are in fact from Rupertus Maldenius, as he appealed for peace in the church in the midst of the Thirty Years War. The 2012 *Book of Discipline of The United Methodist Church*, while not attributing the words to John Wesley, states that they express the spirit of Wesley's views on religious tolerance.

As I completed seminary, I decided to change denominations. My father was the senior pastor of a leading church in a Dallas suburb. After I changed denominations, I became the associate pastor of the church two blocks from where my dad served as pastor. They had Nixons on two corners in that town for two years. I baptized babies, and he did not. People in our community got a kick out of having pastors of these rival churches from one family—since probably many of the families in that community had intermarried between the two congregations. People there had been constantly bringing traditions and beliefs from one church into the other, back and forth, for years.

At first, my theological individuation frustrated my father. It may have even embarrassed him. But then he took a breath and realized that the differences between us were not big enough to impede a mutual and ongoing respect for the other. On the Sundays when I preached, I would see him in the back row at our early service, darting out before the final hymn so he could walk the two blocks back up the street to get ready to lead worship at his congregation. We would meet for lunch a couple times a month and talk shop. It was a great two years.

Even though he and I were able to transcend the theological differences between us, and even though our relationship did not impact either of our churches in any negative way, those two churches did not need to merge! In fact, merging those two congregations would have added distracting and unnecessary complexity to their ministries. Theological multivalence should never be forced—either it works or it doesn't. There were people on his staff that I surely did not want on our staff. And I know he would have felt similarly. The two churches had distinctive cultures and approaches to faith. Each community and each set of leaders needs to pay attention to their limitations for multitheological stretching.

In my exposure to seminary students over the last few years, teaching at Wesley Theological Seminary, I have concluded that most seminarians' capacity for embracing relationship across theological latitude is stronger now than when I was in seminary. There are multiple reasons for this, not the least of which is the cumulative impact from growing up in a society and in families that are increasingly multi-in-almost-every-respect.

In churches where the people bond together around nontheological factors, we may discover greater latitude in theological beliefs, without undermining the glue that holds together the church. Such bonding factors might include:

- a military community;
- a social justice movement;
- a strong relationship to a particular school (either because most of the families have had students there or because a third of the teachers/professors at the school are members of the church);
- a common generational experience as young parents raising small children in a community;
- and a common experience of recovery from addiction.

Think about the place(s) you call church—and the diverse ideas that people hold in tension there. When I served as a pastor week after week and looked out upon the room during worship, I would often note people sharing the same row, joining together in singing—people who sometimes did not know one another as well as I knew them—people who might be challenged to stay in that row if they knew more about each other's ideas. I have heard many pastors of larger congregations make similar observations. It is because of compelling, positive, common experience and conviction that theologically diverse churches hold together. And, because of this, it is a helpful exercise for leaders in such churches to regularly articulate their common ground.

MULTILITURGICAL

It is common practice in many congregations to have at least two styles of worship—and in churches with multiple worship services, significant liturgical differences (beyond music) may appear.

Often we see a simpler order of worship paired with the more modern music style and a more complicated order of worship paired with the more classical music style. This could be considered multiliturgical to some extent—but most "modern" worship gatherings parallel the traditional worship assumptions about sacraments, sermon topic, scripture reading, offering, and so forth. In other words, despite all the so-called worship wars of years past, these two approaches to worship are very easy to run in parallel. I would maintain that one is usually just a certain tweaking of the other.

But what about worship experiences that diverge in paradigm from one another more significantly than music and simplified form? In certain traditions in Europe and North America, extremely innovative forms of church are called Fresh Expressions.[61] Assumptions about what worship includes may expand when

61. The term "Fresh Expressions of Church" is used in Europe among multiple Protestant groups as a category for faith communities, from Lutherans in Germany to almost every denomination in the UK. In the United States, the term is common among certain groups and almost unheard of among others. It is used with different connotations—but in general it is a category for faith communities that color significantly outside the conventional lines of traditional gathering and paradigm in order to relate to nonreligious populations.

significant innovation is involved. I cannot tell you how often I have heard it asked, "Can we count these people in worship attendance for the week?" We count heads for a variety of reasons—but as worship morphs, a third of our flock "gathers" online, and children are in the sanctuary for ten minutes and then in Sunday school—it gets harder to answer the question, "How many folks attended worship at your church last week?" And if you answer with a different set of assumptions than your denominational overseer, you may be accused of cheating in your count![62]

Critical questions regarding worship include:

- Must worship include a sermon by a pastor, expounding in monologue on the scripture and theological idea of the day? What if guided conversation replaces the monologue? Or silent contemplation?
- Must scripture always be read aloud? Is telling a Bible story freestyle sometimes acceptable in lieu of reading the text? How much and what type of scripture is necessary? What if a service contains nothing from the Gospels? What if non-biblical readings become primary in a service's construction?
- Must there be music? A lot of house churches play digital recordings, but no one sings along, given the attendance of six to twelve persons.
- Must money be exchanged? Can worship be separated from the act of giving (which for many of us now happens through online means a few times a year)?

---

62. My interest is far less in counting than in how we define worship—in determining what core elements we believe must be represented in a gathering for it to be Christian worship.

- How many components of worship must be combined in an hour for us to reasonably call it a worship gathering?
- Might we focus on holistic gatherings that transcend categorization as worship, fellowship, or discipleship—but simply contain elements of all?
- What if a gathering contains almost no words? What are the minimal words necessary for a gathering to be claimed as Christian worship? Does a gathering have to be claimed as such in order to be worship?
- What if worship is not just celebrated in the church's gathering, but rather also becomes a part of the challenge as we are sent from the church into the world, a challenge to find two or more folks this week and practice the presence of the Holy together in varied ways?
- Must the gathering last an hour? What about two or three hours? Or forty minutes? What about twenty minutes? Does that count as a "worship service"?
- What if the traditional components of a single worship service are broken up into three or more gatherings?
- Must we gather daily? Weekly? Monthly? What about annually for a three-day festival of faith sharing in varied means?
- Can a pastor consecrate bread and cup across an internet connection? If no ordained pastor is present with the gathering for consecration, does it cease to be Holy Communion?
- Is it possible that our adult children, so many of whom gave up on church as we practice it, never stopped

worshiping? If so, what does that imply as to our understanding of Christian worship?

There are enough questions raised in the preceding list to justify a book just on changing Christian sensibilities about worship. Variance of musical style (our most common focus as we describe how this service varies from that service) barely scratches the surface of the questions around what will confront the church in this century. Liturgical multivalence envisions churches with a wider range of experiences and paradigms related to the experience of coming together consciously into the presence of God.

Each church must articulate what it considers to be the nonnegotiable elements of a worship gathering. This will vary from church to church.[63] High-church Episcopalians and low-church Baptists will come up with different answers. As with other forms of multivalence, divergence of practice is made easier when there are common practices expected in all worship gatherings of a congregation. Churches that are focused mostly on orthodoxy of belief may choose to give considerable latitude around matters of liturgy. But for many churches, integrity of liturgy is critical to their core identity—and such churches will want to spend more time aligning core worship practices between varying services and gatherings.

The Gathering in St Louis is a large church that meets in four locations. On a recent Sunday, they tied their worship gatherings together by theme of the day and also by signage and branding (lots of orange and white, even extended to the color of the chairs). Most notable on this particular day was that each service

---

63. Sometimes this will be defined denominationally, in other cases, at a congregational level.

featured someone teaching the congregation a specific form of contemplative prayer, with scripting very similar from service to service.

The deconstruction of many centuries of European assumptions and sensibilities about worship is just warming up. The worldwide church is in for a very interesting diversification of worship practice in this century—perhaps as interesting as that of the previous twenty centuries combined.

As your church asks itself what core practices define worship within your fellowship, and you consider the questions listed in this section, you will want to think together on multiple planes:

- **Scripting.** Are there particular, exact words that we expect worshipers to hear in each setting? Any scripted words of welcome, announcement, invitation, sacrament?
- **Invitation.** What faith invitation will be offered in each setting—and how will we seek to facilitate meaningful response?
- **Ritual.** What minimum ritual elements do we expect to be included in all gatherings, either identically or contextually adapted? This would include a discussion about practicing sacraments with integrity.
- **Bible.** How does scripture integrate with each gathering and with the flow of gatherings across one, two, or three years?
- **Relationship.** How will we seek to build relationships in and around each gathering—honoring that passing the peace is so much more than a ritual?

5

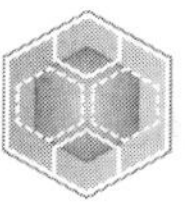

THE CAPACITIES — MULTILOCATIONAL

This chapter reflects on the capacities required for doing ministry in multiple locations as one church. It also considers what happens when a church moves beyond gathering together in physical locations to gathering by digital connection. Expanding a congregation beyond one place of gathering inevitably expands a church's demographic reach and typically raises its multivalence. Many churches seek to treat their expansion beyond a single property as a franchise-like endeavor. They soon discover that it is never quite so simple.

MULTISITE

Multisite is a well-proven strategy of expanding a church's ministry and working past the plateaus in church growth that come from space limitations, geographic limitations, or group dynamics limitations. Multisite congregations do ministry in more than one geographic location, typically including public worship in each place, with a single lead team that oversees the whole network of ministry locations. This is different than the traditional cooperative parish where churches collaborate on certain ministries while retaining significant organizational independence from each other and autonomous lead teams or church boards for each congregation.[64]

A quarter-century into the multisite movement, some things have become quite clear. Perhaps the biggest lesson that is this: the church's leaders have to stay on the same page across the locations. When I recommend multisite strategy to a church, people sometimes ask, "Won't we be two churches if we have two locations?" I tell them the answer has to do almost entirely with the life of the church's leadership team. Many church members will relate primarily to their campus or their worship community. We should expect and accept this. It is the pastors and staff, not the church members, whose alignment primarily defines the church's unity in a multisite arrangement. (This is so crucial that I have devoted the entire next chapter to the topic of leader alignment in a multi church.) There must be good trust and communication habits running both ways between the campus pastor over here

64. It should be noted that the North Carolina Conference of the UMC now organizes its multisite churches as cooperative parishes—where there is one churchwide budget, but where each campus or worship community retains an annual opportunity to pull out of the connection or to renegotiate the terms of connection. Each campus or worship community is organized as a separate congregation in this model but functions covenantally as one. The conference feels that this enables better development of diverse campuses and better develops a leadership community who owns the ministry in each place. I am watching this play out—and may choose to endorse this as an optimal model for multisite ministry, at least within highly connectional denominations.

and the senior pastor and executive pastor back at the mother campus.[65] Pastors need to spend time together: talking vision, working on sermons, doing anything relevant to their common ministry. Without a strong pastoral working relationship, a multisite approach can lead to dis-alignment and a spectacular ministry train crash in slow-mo.

Also, we have learned that owning and managing multiple church properties is not necessary at all—many of the most nimble multisite churches simply borrow or rent space for the time they need it each week. The church I served from 1993 until 2002 added two ministry sites in the latter half of my tenure. In the late 1990s, we spent millions of dollars to buy land and build a facility for a second campus. In 2002, we started a third site by borrowing space from a local restaurant/beach bar, borrowing volunteer musicians from our other worship teams, and borrowing a pastor already on payroll. In other words, our third campus cost almost nothing in startup funding. Millions of dollars versus No Money Down! We were learning (with everyone else) in those early days. The second campus grew to more than a thousand worshipers on a weekend. The third campus grew to around four hundred. While the possibilities for weekday ministry can be enormous in a multiuse facility, the possibilities for multiplication are greater without high startup costs. For this reason, the norm across America for multisite church expansion is borrowed or rented space for

65. Smaller multisite churches may not have an executive pastor, but someone or some group must be equipped and empowered to lead the constant work of alignment between worship communities and common resourcing to such communities. Without this, a multisite can easily become mother campus–centric, treating each new campus as a colony.

a few hours on Sunday or a donated church building that comes with minimal start-up costs. It makes more sense to start quickly and to avoid a capital campaign. When new ministry space comes without a high price tag and the new worship community fills the space, it is easier to move it or simply start another one somewhere else.

In the last decade, with the inspiration of New Life Church in the Chicago area, a trend has developed in which a vital, growing congregation adopts the facilities of congregations that are struggling and near to closing. New Life makes an agreement with the leaders of the dying church to take over total management, to receive the facility at no sales cost, and to welcome any of the remaining members to stay around as part of the new ministries that will be launched.[66] But New Life is clearly in charge. In this way, New Life Church added more than twenty campuses in just a few years, with a critical mass of New Life and neighborhood people ready to flood each renovated property, ready to roll up their sleeves and work. This model costs the multiplying church just a few pennies on the dollar that would be required to build new church buildings everywhere. With no upfront real estate acquisition costs, money is freed up to invest in a skeletal paid staff and critical facility upgrades. It offers the dying church the re-

66. This may seem from a distance like a conquest of a weaker church by a larger church. But in the New Life case, great effort is made to honor the remnant of people in the church that is near to closing and to work at integrating them into the new chapter of ministry at their site. New Life offers a facility takeover as an opportunity to the dying church. Often the dying church initiates these conversations. And they proceed only because the dying church discerns significant advantages for the neighborhood and significant theological affinity with the larger, thriving congregation.

sources it has long needed but failed to get, in order to renew ministry in the neighborhood. Bless a new venue with a launch team of people from one or more of the existing campuses, and it is hard to fail.

As more churches have sought to emulate this adoption model, they discovered that taking shortcuts in the recipe makes for a bad pie.

- A multisite model cannot be replicated without a mother church that possesses a high readiness for reaching and including new people in a new place. Does the church have a recent history of innovating and starting new things that work in reaching new people? If a church has had no adult professions of faith in the last three years and attendance is sagging, it is probably not ready for a multisite challenge. (It could be a time to sell and move or to think about a vital merger.[67])
- The old guard of leaders at the new campus being adopted must relinquish control of the money, the facilities, and the ministry program. New Life has been both gracious and brilliant in their invitation to the people in the dying church to stay around and enjoy the party. But enjoying the party requires the former church leaders letting go of the long meetings, the keys, the money drama—all the control stuff. It is amazing how letting go of all that can

67. See Dirk Elliott's *Vital Merger* (Fun & Done Press, 2013) and Jim Tumberlin's *Better Together* (SanFrancisco: Jossey-Bass, 2012). I define a vital merger as two or more churches coming together, not in order to consolidate and save money, but to free up resources for new ministry development relevant to the community that has emerged in recent years.

spark a spiritual renaissance in a person. Suddenly church participation is about worshiping God, growing spiritually, and serving others without the tedium of running a small business. It is also amazing how keeping the same folks in control can sabotage a fresh start and development of new ministries.

- In some cases, it is helpful to temporarily close the facility to the public (going dark, so to speak), so that renovations can occur and the new ministry can launch fresh with a new brand in the neighborhood. Rushing things on the front end can minimize the ministry potential.
- Arrogance on the part of the mother church's leadership can turn a ministry site adoption quickly into a colonialist mess. A lack of respect for the saints who have labored in a place across many decades or for the distinct cultural context of the neighborhood serves only to wound the people, both those who fought hard to keep the doors open, and their neighbors.
- Not every property is worth saving. A careful study should be made of the mission field and the building condition before assuming that a church building should be adopted as a satellite campus. The church exists to save people and communities, not old buildings.[68] I have worked onsite in more than a thousand churches, and I would say at least half the buildings are not worth saving. In the eastern

68. A helpful variation could be to give a tired church property to a vital church for it to sell, with the understanding that proceeds will be used to start a new ministry presence in the same neighborhood.

United States where some of the buildings are much older, it is common to discover that a property's value is less than the costs of addressing deferred maintenance. We keep old buildings for sentimental reasons, but many have grown impractical from the standpoint of the church's mission. With one church in Southern California, the leaders are selling a building in Fontana and taking the funds to rent space that will be superior to the tired, old building they inherited from the former congregation. Those funds will last for decades.

Any church that is contemplating a move to multisite (of any sort) should give careful thought to a variety of issues. First, is the church's senior leadership ready to tackle this challenge? At least five years' of tenure (with ministry growth) for the senior pastor is advisable prior to a church shifting to a multisite strategy.[69] Additionally, a senior pastor should enter this shift with plans to move nowhere for yet another five years. Without tenures of at least ten years for senior pastors, shifting to a multisite ministry may be ill advised. Also, is the senior pastor temperamentally suited to accept that some of her flock from one place are inevitably going to shift to another place, and be "lost" from the mother campus's worship gatherings and financial base? Such a senior pastor is not discouraged when the new campuses grow faster (and possibly larger) than the mother campus.

---

69. This recommendation originated with my colleague Herb Sadler, the senior pastor of Gulf Breeze United Methodist Church 1975–2003 and 2008–10. The exception to this would be when a church is planted with a multisite vision from the start, such as Urban Village Church in Chicago, in which the first two sites were launched within a year of one another.

Perhaps this is stating the obvious: but this is not a typical senior pastor.[70]

When looking for a pastor to lead a new site, it is always best to start locally. A campus pastor ideally has spent at least two years working with the senior pastor prior to the launch of the new campus. Pastor Steve Cordell of Crosspoint Church in the Pittsburgh area states it rather bluntly: "Cut off your arm before hiring a campus pastor from outside your church." Furthermore, the senior pastor and the local church lead team choose this pastor, not a long-distance ecclesial authority.[71] Highly credentialed pastors who come from outside the local church's culture may be challenged to build a partnership with a senior pastor, to get on the page of the local church's ministry philosophy, and to plant well at the same time. They look good on paper resumes, but they don't know the local culture, and they often are not eager to learn it or, when needed, to defer to it. Pastors new to the community may lack the local credibility to gather a team of leaders quickly for launch of the new campus.

In the interest of higher multivalence and nimbleness at each campus, I recommend that senior pastors trust campus pastors and their teams to make the decisions as often as possible about

---

70. Often this pastor's ego security has been established over the years as she or he led in the growth of church and worship communities. Now, faced with a multisite challenge, they no longer feel the need to prove their leader competency by convening the largest worship crowd.

71. There is virtually unanimous agreement among senior pastors of multisite churches that the local church must choose their own campus pastors. Bishops and supervisory authorities: beware. You are asking for wasted money, a high degree of conflict, and failed campuses when you impose people into campus leadership from outside the culture of a multisite church. Please do not sabotage the churches that are most likely to grow and to offer vitality to your region!

the ministry challenges and questions on their campus. Decide what is to be standardized across the church, and then trust the site management! A playbook for how decisions are to be made and conflicts are to be resolved can be helpful. Several of the larger multisite churches have developed these, and they are often happy to share with others. The decisions can range from how worship is planned to how salaries are set: the clearer the protocols, the easier for everyone! Procedural systems must shift to reflect the playbook.[72]

Campus pastors, like all church planters, need to spend major chunks of time in their community context—and to live near their campus when at all possible.[73] Scott Chrostek of Church of the Resurrection in Leawood, Kansas, insists that the majority of a campus pastor's time be spent in their neighborhood or community context—in the focal missional zone of their campus, building community in that zone.

The campus pastor should be the undisputed staff team captain at their campus. When a children's ministry director at the new campus hears one thing from the children's ministry team

---

72. The mother campus typically has multiple staff members in administrative capacities, executing procedures that were designed for the mother campus. Some of these staff (housed in offices at the mother campus) will shift to a role serving all campuses. Subjecting a new campus to the same deadlines or protocols as the mother campus can slow down the innovation and creativity of the new campus. Changes will be required.

73. It is common for family issues or cost of housing to make it difficult for a planting pastor to live in the neighborhood where the ministry startup is focused. Sometimes, we have to work with such constraints. But church planters that have to commute in and out of their parish area typically see slower ministry growth in the early years. Often, hindsight reveals that it would have been better to just add $15,000 to the pastor's housing allowance from the start, so that he could live in the heart of the parish zone.

at the mother campus and another thing from the campus pastor, the campus pastor's opinion takes precedence. If that creates a church alignment problem, the senior pastor (or executive pastor overseeing campuses) and the campus pastor can iron out the issues, reporting their consensus recommendation to the children's ministry team church-wide.

When the church's unified website is not serving the campus adequately, the campus pastor must be empowered to see to it that reasonable accommodation is made—possibly a link to another site or to a customized campus landing page, designed with the campus's constituency in mind.[74] If branding confusion arises in this pursuit, let the senior pastor (or executive pastor) and campus pastor sort through the challenge first, and then they can work it out with communications and web team(s) as an aligned pastoral team.

A feisty campus pastor speaking up for their campus should not be seen as disloyal! Pastor Adam Weber of Embrace Church puts it this way, "Campus pastors must fight for their campus. Speak up in meetings. Communicate what things you're seeing that the bigger church and central staff are not seeing." As a guy who has coached plenty of campus pastors, I say, "Amen, Adam!"

On the flip side, campus pastors have to navigate a necessary tension: they are in the lead on their campus, but often second, third, or fourth chair in the larger church organization. Scott Chrostek reminds campus pastors that a lot of the decision-making authority resides elsewhere. Flexibility is in order. They

---

74. Unified websites can be a challenge for multisite churches unless they are pursuing an almost franchise-like sameness from campus to campus. The values of common branding and creative freedom must be weighed in each case. Achieving the church's mission must be the primary consideration.

will often have to roll with decisions that are not their first preference. Herb Sadler, who served Gulf Breeze Church for more than three decades, says, "Every campus pastor must be committed (first) to the whole church and not just their campus."

If the church grows to four or more campuses, the need for shifting strategy in senior church leadership becomes more acute. It is often wise to select a campus pastor for the mother campus other than the senior pastor, so that the latter is not expected to be a movement leader and an effective campus pastor simultaneously. Occasionally I see a senior pastor who enjoys the challenge of a start-up going out to become the planting pastor of the new campus. The work of planting a new site is intense. If done well, it requires that senior pastor to pull loose from certain responsibilities; new staffing hours must be added to cover those responsibilities.

When the senior pastor moves or retires, I recommend looking first for a successor within the current pastoral team. One of most dangerous passages for any multisite church is when the senior pastor transitions out and a new one enters. The pastoral alignment must be rebuilt at that time—if not, bad things will ensue.

There must be a strong central capacity for logistics and execution within the church's ministry team. Often this capacity is connected with a competent executive pastor or director of operations. In smaller congregations, this executive function is sometimes less developed or missing altogether. It may be part of the role of senior pastor.[75] In a multisite church, the

75. If a senior pastor intends to be hands-on in the development of new campuses, then I would recommend that there be a highly competent executive assistant for such a pastor.

senior pastor can't lead effectively while worrying about stackable chairs or sound system upgrades. I once recommended a young church to add an executive pastor when they were starting to hit four hundred in worship attendance, not because of their church size but because of the impending increase in church operational complexity as they added new worship locations.

One person within the church administrative structure should be designated as the clear point of connection for each campus pastor. With several campuses, this connector could warrant a full-time job. This relationship is as critical as the relationship between the campus pastor and the senior pastor. If decisions at the mother campus come as a surprise to the campus pastor, there will be a problem.[76]

Launching worship prematurely means that we do not yet have enough human beings attached to the new campus to (1) cover the volunteer bases necessary for a functional Sunday ministry—reasonably forty persons with Sunday responsibilities, (2) gather enough people that there is reasonable energy in the worship service—at least eighty adults in the room during the first ten minutes of the service, and (3) gather enough people to achieve the minimum critical mass of twenty-five elementary age

---

76. As a campus pastor 1999–2002, I was part of all staffing conversations and hiring decisions for my campus. When they decided to swap our lead custodian with another from the team at the mother campus, I was in the loop about the change and about why they were doing it. When our growth plateaued for lack of parking, I made an appeal to add a gravel overflow lot with general church funds, and I had expanded parking in less than two months. In short, we worked as one church to grow ministry on each campus, and we treated the issues at what was then our newest campus with the same seriousness of the issues at the mother campus. As a result, the new campus grew!

children.[77] At least 50 percent more than these minimums are needed on the launch Sunday itself. So if the goal is one hundred attendees on average in the first year, we should be planning for 150 or more on opening day.[78]

The leaders who form the launch team for the new campus must be well organized in advance. Some will need to leave a campus where their leadership has been critical and deeply valued. Others will step up to leadership in the new campus in ways that they did not display before. If a person feels led to go with the new team, no one should stop them, especially not a senior pastor or campus pastor who wants to hold on to their financial pledge.

Launch team members should be challenged to a very high level of personal commitment. Ken Nash of Watermark Church near Buffalo, New York, believes that highly committed laity can tackle almost every challenge of a new campus with minimal pastoral involvement, so long as they have been challenged to a high bar of personal commitment—including financial commitment. He would remind us that many of our churches are loaded with talent and life experience, gifts that are often overlooked in terms of church leadership.

---

77. With small venues, you can scale this back a bit, since you are not trying to grow it past two hundred attendees. But even with small venues, in most cases you would want a minimum of sixty persons per week in the big room during the first ten minutes of the service, thirty workers onsite (mostly volunteers) and fifteen kids grade school age. With house churches and micro venues, critical mass is whatever feels good in a living room or a small pub.

78. Often the opening day brings twice the number we can expect on a weekly basis in the first year. After the first campus I planted launched with 590 on day one, we then averaged around 325 per Sunday over the first year. These ratios have not changed much over time.

Campus financial sustainability is critical. If you start it, plan to fund it . . . over and above the income the new campus will generate for a few years. Greg McKinnon suggests that multisite churches think in terms of subsidy for four years (reducing the subsidy annually). Adam Weber emphasizes that the campus pastor must be committed on the other end to develop stewardship and to create a workable ministry plan that is within the community's financial reach. Even with low-income populations, there is benefit to minimizing the campus subsidy as much as possible—it just keeps a healthy working relationship between campuses. If a campus pastor serves a poor population, perhaps the mother church can fund the pastor's salary in part by adding some sort of church-wide leadership responsibility to the pastor's portfolio. In this way, the campus does not have to fund the entire salary.[79]

The style and demographic makeup of the worship services may vary considerably, but it is advisable to observe defined common ground between the services. This common ground may be expressed in any the following ways:

- One preacher for the weekend, preaching live in at least one venue, with large screen video presentation of the sermon in the other venues.[80]

---

79. Even with a one-budget-for-the-whole-church model (recommended), it is important for church leadership to keep an eye on the relative costs of each campus and/or worship community versus their income.

80. Scott Chrostek of Church of the Resurrection points out that preachers whose sermons are to be used across multiple campuses must shift their preaching style to speak to a more global audience, relating the message in ways that can be adapted to a variety of community contexts.

- Multiple preachers for the weekend, preaching similar themes and biblical texts, adjusting presentation details to the context of each location.[81]
- All of the campus pastors meeting two or three hours weekly (or biweekly) for prayer, ministry planning, and fellowship.
- Strategies for preventing triangulation, which would include scripted responses to certain questions and statements, mutually agreeable across the church's lead team and pastoral team.
- Usage of a single set of church logos, key words, core values, or other common branding components.
- Common branding or other protocols and values in children's ministry. For example: there may be a Promised Land[82] children's ministry at each venue—similar to the way that there is a Windjammer buffet on every Royal Caribbean cruise ship in the world, despite the differences in the ships and the populations served.
- Church-wide emphases around particular ministry events, mission projects, or seasonal focus—so that if a person attended different campuses from week to week, the overall narrative of the church's ministry life would be coherent.

Multisite churches vary in terms of the degree of uniformity expressed from campus to campus. The more franchise-like a

---

81. If ethnic, gender, or generational diversity are important values, then a church may choose to focus on developing a larger preaching team, modeling such diversity in the pastoral team, rather than to just broadcast a single excellent preacher to the worship sites.
82. This is just an example of a random brand name for a children's ministry.

church's approach, the more ministry procedures that can be standardized across all campuses, and the more functions that can be centralized. Some of the largest multisite churches are known for highly uniform procedures church-wide. They are not necessarily known for the other kinds of multivalence. For a church that seeks a highly contextualized and customized ministry at each location, it would be a bad idea to model its multisite practices after a more uniform church.

If a church wants to add a campus with a different ethnic focus than currently exists, or if a church seeks to become multiethnic and multisite simultaneously, I would say, "Be very careful." Proceed cautiously, especially if the host culture is white, in order to avoid a colonialist dynamic, complete with intense conflict, hurt feelings, and alienated leaders. In such a case, I would recommend using the Intercultural Development Inventory with the church leader team.[83]

Finally, if your church's valence is already pretty high, think carefully about whether you wish to further ratchet up the complexity of holding together as one church. Do you really want to expand your juggling act to multiple locations? There are times when it makes sense to just plant another church and bless them to organize their ministry independently.

MULTIDIGITAL GATHERING

I was driving in northern Virginia one Sunday morning a couple years back to make a site visit to a church I was coaching. As I flipped through radio stations, I came to an NPR show on which

83. Each IDI report comes with guidance on how to improve individual and corporate competencies for intercultural partnerships.

Paul Rauschenbusch was interviewing Diana Butler Bass. The question I recall him asking, in fact the only thing I remember of the interview is "Diana, where is the church going to be in fifty years?" Her answer was succinct: "On the internet."[84] This is an important and prophetic word for us all to hear.

Now, in almost no time, a colleague and I are working with two different pastors in northern Virginia where we are unable even to make a Sunday site visit. Both pastors are planting virtual communities. I can visit the local team, but the best way to visit the church is to get a cup of coffee, open my laptop, and log on.

Notably, a major denominational body put big money in the game for each of these churches, offering the full package of new church start-up funding, just as they would have done for a new church meeting in a high school gymnasium.[85] Time will tell whether these communities will take root as self-sustaining ventures. We assume that the per capita giving will not be as much per person as with a church physically gathered—and yet one of the two is (as of this writing) a year ahead of schedule on its benchmarks toward financial self-sustainability. In any case, welcome to the church where your small group leader is stationed in Iraq and the newest member of that group may live in Australia.

First United Methodist Church of Williamsport, Pennsylvania, has experimented with a biweekly "Kitchen Convo" video

---

84. Paul Rauschenbush interview with Diana Butler Bass, archived in the *All Together* podcast, May 29, 2015. This was following the publication of her book *Grounded: Finding God in the World: A Spiritual Revolution* (New York: HarperCollins, 2015).

85. The Virginia United Methodists gave these two grants in 2017. And now that I have named them in this way, I am almost certain that one or two others will contact me to say they gave full funding earlier.

recording, with two of their pastors in barstools in one of their kitchens, studying a Bible passage and sharing in a robust conversation about the life implications. It provides an easy way for a person to share faith with a friend, simply to send the link to that person or several of their Facebook contacts. Moreover, because Kitchen Convo is broadcast via Facebook Live, it is possible for viewers to comment, ask questions, or follow up in a private conversation with a leader at the church. After just a couple months, the piece was getting six hundred views each week and rising—not a bad attendance for a weekly Bible study in a church of eight hundred average worship attendees! Later they changed the format to include interviews, and the views spiked up over a thousand. The majority of the viewers were not physically present in a First UMC worship gathering the preceding Sunday.

And it costs nothing other than the time to prepare for it each week.

We are likely to see an explosion of online ministry bigger than the multisite revolution of twenty-five years ago. Some of the factors driving this:

- Big screen high definition TVs with internet access. It makes a difference in one's online experience when you are no longer working off a 13-inch computer screen, but on nearly the entire south wall of your living room, with surround sound.
- Online conferencing technology is rapidly advancing, so that connections are more stable and dependable. Furthermore, it is hard to go to college or to work without having to engage such technology for online interaction (and get accustomed to it).

- Almost everyone under the age of sixty today began adapting to computers before the age of thirty (and, in so doing, entered the digital culture). Ironically, this is exactly the same population that has dropped off the radar of most historic congregations.
- As for people under thirty, most of them came to consciousness as children with digital devices in their hands. Their whole concept of virtuality is changing—in some cases disappearing. Experience is real—in all sorts of modes. This segment of the population finds itself profoundly disengaged and disconnected from their parents' churches.
- Major personal relationships start online these days. Why not church relationships? I predict that the majority of today's children may meet their future spouse via the internet. For increasing numbers of people, online is just another great way of meeting—as real as if the people were physically in the same room.

It is perhaps still too early to see the full contours of what is emerging. But online capabilities and ministry design will be more than simply a nuance on how we do church. Digital ministry is paradigm-disruptive.

I expect that as we live more fully into the digital age, there will be decreased emphasis on video presentation of worship experiences created for a crowd gathered together physically, and more worship and interactive possibilities designed entirely for and with people on the web. Twenty-first-century people are embracing relationship and interactivity with passion, even as they are becoming less engaged with passive and institutional expressions of faith, art, education, and other cultural experiences.

I also would expect increased user-customization of the experience and more unmonitored and unauthorized interactions within church-created platforms. The creation of online spiritual theme parks will encourage people to roam freely and to ride whatever they wish . . . even to design their own ride and share it with others.

The implications are big, and the valence required to do multi-digital well—enormous!

Saddleback Church in Southern California, a conservative megachurch, is currently the curator of the online ministry most often referenced within my ministry circles. It is good to keep an eye on what such churches are learning. The theology of Saddleback would be problematic for many of the folks reading this book. However, their most relevant learning is related to people dynamics and technology—both of which are largely atheological. While large organizations have the resources to invest, and often take the lead early-on when paradigm shifts are underway, it is fair to expect that the scale of this revolution will soon overtake Saddleback's ability to absorb and manage it, without finally pulling back in defense of their existing ministry paradigm. For this reason, I would expect the most significant future innovations related to church and online connections to come from an up-start player—someone or some new church on the margins—people with nothing to lose if online church quickly surpasses church-as-we-have-known-it.

6

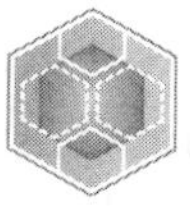

THE LEADER TEAM

As goes the leader team, so goes the church.

Every capacity for multi ministry we wish to develop within a church should first be well developed within the life of the leader team. Period. Anything we want our church to be good at, our leaders should be better at! Lots of churches may say they want to embrace a multi vision—but have their leaders yet done the work to make it possible?

The challenge of building a multi kind of team is so much more than simply getting the right people in the room. These people have to learn how to work together in ways that are truly multi—where all voices can be heard and where prayerful consensus can emerge. This doesn't happen overnight. As they live into a multi life as a team, they will encounter bumps and tensions that they must learn how to navigate. Getting to the point where we are comfortable enough with one another that team members feel that they can push back on ideas without creating offense—that is a sweet tipping point.

Not everyone who comes on the team will stay on the team. Feelings will get hurt. Apologies will be required. Self-awareness will increase. This kind of team takes work to form, and even more work to hold together as it grows in its power and grace.

Patience is in order—and the continued reminder that an infinitely higher valence is not the point.

Whatever good we seek to create in the life of the church overall must be developed first on a small scale in the life of the leader community, and (with time) we can expect it to spread. For example:

- Churches that have historically functioned as worship gatherings with light fellowship attached can become churches of small groups, with a deeper commitment to the spiritual journey of each person—if the leaders are willing to make this shift themselves first and then to rework the covenant of expectations for new leaders around the shift.
- Churches that have historically focused primarily on spiritual inspiration can become churches of profound mission and community service—if the leaders agree to begin spending time serving their neighbors beyond the church walls as a component and expectation of spiritual leadership.
- Churches that have been primarily monoethnic can become multiethnic—if they are willing to morph the leader team into a functional multiethnic body.
- Even in churches with a flat structure, where persons from the margins of the church are encouraged to initiate, to challenge, and to innovate, life at the leader table is critical! In this case, the leader table must open itself to transformative encounter with persons from outside their circle on a

continual basis. Old-school, closed-system, top-down can't lead a flat structure.

It really is this simple. Show me a team of leaders united in vision and resolve—leaders who dare as a team to live into their vision with consistent action and integrity, leaders who do not panic and fold when a few of the old guard attack them for changing the rules—and I will show you a wider transformation soon to occur within their church, and probably already underway.

On the flip side: any attitude, habit, or behavior that could sabotage a church's vision becomes lethal when it sets up camp inside the leader team. When dysfunction infects the leader community, we may be tempted to think it won't show—and perhaps it won't show publicly at first. But bad system dynamics are as contagious as the flu. You don't have to show symptoms of the flu to give it to me! When the leaders are out of sync with the stated vision (or out of sync with each other), the vision is effectively blocked.

It is common in churches to have some leaders who resist any kind of transformation desired for the church. Such resistance must be addressed. Not every vision is for everybody. But once a vision has been embraced, leaders need to live into the vision—or step out of leadership. This is doubly true for paid leaders! Triply true for pastors!

Why pay someone to subvert the direction of the whole? Why keep a volunteer in leadership who resents the church's vision? The answer typically is to avoid conflict. But if the church has chosen a direction, retaining a leader who is actively at odds with the direction is not conflict avoidance—it is the choice to remain mired in conflict. And an ongoing conflict will surely subvert the vision.

In multivalence theory, whenever a loose electron is left without a constructive role in the bonding between atoms, that electron begins to repel and subvert the bonds that hold the whole molecule together. Transferring that idea to church leadership: a staff member or other influential leader who is not working for the whole is probably working against it, whether they are conscious of this or not.

This can be tough in situations where certain long-time employees or church members signed onto the vision in another era, perhaps when the church was smaller or when it operated with a different set of ground rules. We can be sympathetic to the long-time leader and still address the situation constructively. Their discomfort with the change is real: they are being asked to buy into a vision at odds with how they have operated across the years, and possibly to lead in ways in which they are not gifted.

For those staff who cannot adjust to new expectations, given new ministry conditions and possibly new core values, there are a few options.

- Grant them a reasonable (and clearly defined) amount of time to find a new job, with the proviso that they remain cheerful in their day-to-day work and promise to speak no ill of the church leadership or vision in any conversation. Mature Christian servants are often up to the challenge!
- If the issues are less about core values and more about critical skills, we may be able to find them a new place on our team (or not).
- Choose to bring their time of service to an end immediately, with some severance package.

Many long-tenured staff persons have a cheering section within the congregation, and possibly within the staff itself—so termination presents a risk of conflict and disruption in church life. Often a church has to move carefully, and sometimes more slowly than they would prefer. It is best when a lay-led personnel team, having already bought into the new vision and covenants, can supervise an exit plan. It may be necessary to downsize and/or shift payroll expenses around to other areas, but indefinitely retaining staff members who are off-vision, ill-equipped, or possibly too expensive for the challenges of change is almost never a good option.

Managing volunteer leaders at odds with vision is trickier than managing staff leaders. The very nature of an employee-employer relationship means that accountability is defined. It is seldom so defined for volunteers. But everyone needs to get on board: all the leaders—including those who are not on payroll. Covenants can be developed so that as leaders' terms expire, new leaders come on with reasonable buy-in to the vision, values, and practices that are deemed central to the church's life.

GET ME OFF THIS LEADER TEAM!

If I am a leader within my church, and I find myself at odds with my church's vision or some of its critical decisions, my best option may be to step out of leadership at the first good opportunity and continue to engage in church life wherever I find it personally fulfilling. Can I find a graceful exit ramp off the team and pursue another job or area of service? Are my relationships with my sisters and brothers in the church worth more to me than winning on a particular issue? Does my family find the church to be a life-giving place? If the answer is yes to any of those questions, I should move very carefully and prayerfully as I respond to a church direction with which I disagree.

Once I am out of leadership, I might be able to get more out of worship and to increase my personal investment in a ministry team where I have gifts and passion. Leadership can be exercised at so many different altitudes in ministry. The longer I have been out of a pastoral leadership role personally, the further I prefer to sit from governance committees and teams dealing with finances or large systems. I don't want or need to control the church. It will never be perfect, anyway. I just want to live and serve (and sometimes lead) on the frontlines and see the ministry action.

If the issues at play in the vision-shift are so painful for me that I am tempted to lead a holy war within the congregation, I had best pray long and hard before acting. Perhaps it is better for everyone (including my family) if I simply find another church to call home!

So what specifically might we ask of our church's leaders, as we live more fully into a vision of multi? What kinds of behaviors might we include in leadership covenants. I would like to suggest eight habits. (These habits hold true for churches of all sizes, although some of the examples below reflect the experience of large systems.)

HABIT 1. COMMITMENT TO THE PRACTICES

The practices in chapter 2 are foundational to the life of the leader community of a multichurch and should be encouraged throughout the church body. Chapter 2 could be a helpful chapter for church leaders (staff and lay) to study together. The ways that spiritual practices and disciplines play out for particular teams can vary endlessly. Look for methods that feel contextually appropriate to your team. The way that the lead team at Calvary Baptist Church prays together may be markedly different from the way the team prays together at Trinity Presbyterian Church.

A team covenant can provide specific expectations for these practices: forms of prayer, a one-on-one accountability partner, participation in church life (worship, groups, etc.), servanthood (volunteer participation in a humble role regularly), and protocols of respectful communication and conflict management. Depending on the type(s) of multi that has captured the team's interest for church-wide focus, there could be prescribed practices challenging leaders and members to develop personal friendships across certain kinds of human frontiers (geographic, faith-related, ethnic, etc.).

Keep any covenant simple—just a few key practices that are compelling for the months ahead. You don't need to include every virtue in the Bible! That's too much. Remember, the leaders are setting footsteps for the whole church to follow. Keep it focused. Keep it doable. The practices that you lift up are simply gateways into other kinds of activity and service that will develop as God's grace makes deeper inroads into people's lives.

Also, review the covenant regularly as a leader team. Do some things together as a team to keep the covenant alive—otherwise it will become just another irrelevant document on the church's computer drive.[86]

HABIT 2. ATTENTION TO AFFINITY

Julian Davies defined affinity as "the relative ease with which certain particles will bond with each other."[87] It has long been noted that affinity is of critical importance between any ministry leader and the population they seek to lead, especially if the population has not yet been gathered into a group or a church, and

86. See Kim Shockley and Paul Nixon, Chapter 8, "Holding Difficult People Accountable" in *The Surprise Factor* (Nashville: Abingdon Press, 2013).

87. Julian Davies interview, December 27, 2017.

any two or more ministry partners that are seeking to work in tandem and as a team.

Such affinity is worth monitoring even when there is relative homogeneity (sameness of people) in the church or between the church and the community. As a church seeks to increase its valence, affinity becomes even more critical, and, likely, more challenging.

At the most basic level, affinity may be based upon shared experiences or shared values. Shared experiences might include growing up in a small Texas town, for example, or emigrating from Vietnam. Shared values may be found across diverse life experiences. As a pastor, I discovered an affinity for military officers—even though I never served in the military—appreciating their skills in critical thinking, their understanding of procedure and planning, their willingness to serve without great personal accolade, and their cross-cultural capacities from having worked within a multivalent system—and, in many cases, their well-developed compassion as persons who have carried responsibility for the lives of others.

An affinity based on shared values only grows stronger when paired with shared experience. As a person who has started several small businesses, I always seem to find good energy when I get in a room with people who have also started things, all kinds of things. I have affinity for starters. When I think of my years as a leader within the Church Planting Team of the United Methodist Church[88]—a team of considerable diversity—I realize that most of us who have served on the team are starters and planters. This commonality has helped our team bond across the years.

---

88. Sometimes called "Path 1," the Community Engagement and Church Planting Team is a part of Discipleship Ministries, a general agency of The United Methodist Church.

STOP AND THINK

Who are some of the people for whom you have affinity? What kinds of groups of people? What kinds of people outside the church? Thinking beyond yourself, what are your ministry team's affinities? What about your church: what kinds of people energize your church and thus are easy to reach?[89]

Affinity also touches upon factors that are intangible and hard to identify. This is why churches, when interviewing new staff from outside the church system, may choose to have the candidate interact with others on the team, just to observe synergy and affinity. If there is an awkwardness or a lack of obvious affinity between the new person and the staff, the interview team can explore what that is about, especially before inviting someone to move five hundred miles and to relocate their family. Otherwise, the risk may be a short tenure and loss of ministry momentum.

Not everyone on a leader team experiences affinity toward every other person. But paying attention to the affinity of the team for each person, and for the ways that they bond to the team, is essential. This is in addition to the affinity that each ministry leader must develop with the teams they lead and the constituencies they seek to serve.

89. Mission Insite (missioninsite.com) offers a Comparative Insite report in which the primary Mosaic Lifestyle groups of the congregation's population are compared with that of the community around it. I find this to be helpful to congregations as they seek to articulate who they are best-equipped to reach and serve—and as they seek to define how they desire to stretch their social bandwidth.

HABIT 3. CULTIVATING SPIRITUAL MATURITY

This equates to lowering our need for homogeneity. Human beings can expand our range of affinities over time as we are exposed to more kinds of people and to their varied experiences. We can seek to do our best in serving and partnering with a wide assortment of people across the decades. But there are limits to this. There will be plenty such people for whom we simply don't ever feel a lot of affinity. This is normal. Yet, as we grow spiritually, we may discover deep blessing and satisfaction in working with certain people with whom we feel little natural connectedness.

Paul's words "There is no longer Jew or Greek . . . slave or free . . . male or female, for all of you are one in Christ Jesus" speak most obviously to our equal status in the family of God, which transcends human constructs of power and insider/outsider. These words also speak to affinity. There will always be persons with whom we have little in common and who may not be naturally interesting to us, and yet we perceive that God is calling us to be one with them, not just in theory, but in action, in worship, and in breaking bread.

Of the four areas measured in the Readiness 360 project, there is one area that has been discovered to be distinctive: as it strengthens, it can drive strengthening in the other three areas. That area is spiritual intensity, dealing with the vitality of a person's (and a church's) walk with God. You can strengthen any of the other areas with modest to little impact that is shared across the spectrum. But as people grow spiritually, their relational skills tend to improve, their capacity increases for loving people from other cultural orientations, and they are more likely to put self-interest aside in aligning with ministry directions for the good of the whole.

Highly effective churches expect their leaders to demonstrate spiritual maturity, beginning with participation in core spiritual practices, as discussed earlier. It extends to evidence of maturity in how they relate to others on the team, how they work for the unity of the body and seek to diffuse discord. They hold their leaders, paid and unpaid, accountable in terms of where and how they are seeking to grow in their understanding of God's will and their practice of faith.

HABIT 4. TIME IN RELATIONSHIP

Recall Sam Rodriguez' observation: In a multi kind of church, it's all about relationship.

A team needs relationship development time before being asked to tackle the pressures of leading a multivalent ministry advance for the church. The higher the valence, the more critical such time becomes! This may be relationship prior to doing ministry together or having served together on a ministry team. It could mean a camping trip with hiking and canoeing for several days. Some church staffs go out one day each week for lunch, just to relax, turn off work, and enjoy one another's company. Others take retreat time to get away overnight, not just to work but to play, to get in the kitchen together, to watch a movie, and so on. The team that doesn't play and hang together well probably doesn't get to know one another very well. Relationship is fundamental for teaming. Add in two or three dimensions of multi and it becomes supremely critical: it's a key part of the glue that holds the molecule together. In relationship, we discover our human commonality—and from there, all kinds of new configurations of tribes or locations become possible.

When I was in fifth grade, my teacher asked me to befriend a boy in my class named Shawn. Shawn brought multivalent challenges to my world that included race, socioeconomic culture, and academics. I had the best grades in the class and Shawn had some of the lowest. This teacher's gift in jump-starting a friendship offered both Shawn and me the discovery that there is a world of possibility beyond sameness. In our friendship that year, there was some exchange of skills—he taught me how to stand up to a bully and I helped him with math. But mostly I just remember that we had fun, the way fifth graders do: outdoors, without overthinking stuff, playing games and telling stories.

In 2005, I watched a married couple (he was from Alabama and she was from Venezuela) help to form a new church in Mobile. The church was bilingual from the very first meeting in the pastor's living room.[90] This couple was not a pastoral team—they were members of the launch team. Their relationship and accumulated experience as a multilingual and multiethnic family helped set the DNA of the emerging church. It has been widely noted that multiethnic churches often begin with multiethnic families within their leadership.

The component of cultural openness, which can be measured with Readiness 360, is directly impacted by the accumulated multivalent relationships of the people in the church—at work, at home, at school, in their community activities. For this reason, cultural openness will typically be the most undeveloped capacity for churches in very homogenous contexts, while it may be a highly developed capacity in a Los Angeles or Houston congregation.

Such more homogeneous churches would be wise to work on theological and ethnic multivalence first, before attempting

90. The church is called the Grace Place/la Plaza de Gracia. It was, from its early days, a relatively small congregation with a high valence.

to manage diversity in multiple locations. This is especially true if there is significant ethnic difference between the two neighborhoods where they will have ministry sites.

If (by chance) the church is historically white or historically black, we just added another level of difficulty. White people all over the world have been conditioned to try to get their way—even when they don't know they are doing it. In terms of African American host culture—the black church has been a fortress amid the struggles for human dignity in North America during the last four centuries. For a historically black church in America to shift to a multiethnic culture is going to change the nature of the nurturing fortress people experience there. And beyond that, if white persons are part of the intended mix, there is the challenge of getting white persons to consider a historically black church as a live option for themselves. The church's lead team must live into what it means to be a community of black and white persons on a spiritual journey together. As they work through this and see ministry growing in a single location with team practices of trust and respect, then they can proceed to do ministry in two locations.

Let's say that a church wishes to be multitheological, multiethnic, and multisite. That could present a complicated juggling act. For a church to pull it off, the leaders must first be able to juggle these things within their leader community with some degree of skill. This would mean that the team must possess a significant range of theological approaches and have found a comfortable alliance that transcends differences of style or belief. Plus the team must have an ethnic mix that would approximate what one might see at the nearby shopping mall—or at least that would model the degree of intermix that the church feels is doable for now.

HABIT 5. TEAM FIRST

"If the team wins, I win."

This is essential. Some people are not ready to define their success as the success of this team and its mission. There have to be reasons why this team winning would represent a win for one personally, at this place in their life. Otherwise, this simply isn't their team.

There is nothing wrong with a person acknowledging that a particular team is not for them. No one needs to waste their time and others' time in needless tug-of-war or other efforts that yield little that is productive. There are so many teams out there. Why stay on a team where one is misaligned or where their gifts cannot be meaningfully engaged? This is not to say that all of a person's gifts have to be engaged on any team—but is this a team where they can make a good difference and help contribute to a win?

At one level, it is essential that a person share the vision and values of the team—I would even go so far as to say that it is essential that one is passionate about the vision and values. But even if all of that aligns, they may not jibe with the varied personalities or other idiosyncrasies of the team. For example, the team may ask a person to work in a busy office when they really are more effective in quiet space. The team may not offer adequate opportunity for using the gifts that a person desires to use. A person may wish to work with more (or less) autonomy than is prescribed. There may be a personality or two that annoys a person to the degree that they are constantly distracted from where they need to focus. The ministry system that the team manages may be larger than one would prefer, or smaller.

In our conversation on multivalence, Julian Davies noted that "big, bulky things don't bond easily—they sometimes get in the way." Outsized ego is a big, bulky thing. Recall the old cliché from B-grade 1950s western movies: "There's not enough room in these here parts for both you and me." When it comes to ministry teams, how often this can be said! If participation on a team is constantly frustrating, resolve it quickly. Or move on!

Some folks carry too strong a vision and opinion on how things should run to work within a context where their opinion is marginalized. Failure to get comfortable on a team should not be seen as a personality flaw. It's just not the right team—that's all we can safely say. There are plenty of highly entrepreneurial senior pastors who once found themselves miserable on somebody else's team. They got off those teams and found other teams, where (to use Jim Collins' famed term) they found "the right seat on the bus."[91] And often that was the driver's seat! Good for them—good for all of us!

One brief clarification: to put the team ahead of self is never a request for blind loyalty. There are certain situations where we may see things that run counter to the team's stated mission—and where the adage applies: "if you see something, please say something!" Loyalty to a team should never be equated with silence when we stumble upon unethical behavior or practices that clearly run counter to the church's stated mission and values.

HABIT 6. TRUST THAT RUNS TWO DIRECTIONS

As healthy team dynamics are built, trust grows. It is important that trust runs in two directions in a church with a multi ministry. The leaders must be able to trust the senior pastor, and also to trust their personal team leader or supervisor if that person is

---

91. Jim Collins, *Good to Great*, (New York: Harper Business, 2001).

other than the senior pastor. In turn, the people at the top of the management hierarchy must be able to trust the ministry managers that they have deployed to lead.

Every ministry department and/or project needs a leader. So does every ministry location. Sometimes, these roles can be shared, but typically there are individual persons named as leaders at various places throughout a multivalent church's ministry. Such leaders take clear responsibility for anything that happens in their realm of ministry oversight.

Once when I was a campus pastor, a door to one of our preschool classrooms was left unlocked. Some middle school students got into the room later that day and found a camera that the teacher used for capturing special moments throughout the school year. They used the camera to take pictures of body parts, and then left the camera. When the teacher went to develop the roll of film, the photos caused us to reassess our building security procedures. We wanted to maintain a safe ministry space. That same year, a homeless man quietly, invisibly, moved into the attic of our building, slowly collecting all his earthly possessions up there, including a decent wardrobe arranged nicely on hangers. How he pulled this off remains a mystery. As the campus pastor, I had to take responsibility for responding to these situations. A church member who was a hotel manager taught us protocols for monitoring safety in a complex public space. We began a practice of hourly walk-throughs by designated staff members or volunteers during any period of time when the building was open to the public—a much more intense protocol of building security than was practiced at our church's original campus. Our response as a campus team to such situations helped us to retain a high degree of trust from the senior church leadership.

Just as critical in the maintenance of trust was the fact that our ministries at that campus were steadily growing, even outpacing the benchmarks we had set for ourselves. As trust increased in our management, more freedom was given to make decisions without running everything up the flagpole to a higher authority.

Additionally, it was important that our campus leadership demonstrate that we were team players with the larger church. One time, the church cancelled all services at both locations to have a joint worship experience at a large theater downtown. I knew that this would leave scores of people coming to both campuses that Sunday, only to discover that the church had moved several miles away that week. I thought this was a bad idea, in terms of our relationship with the public. I was overruled. And that was that. I got on board and supported the church-wide gathering at the theater—and we had a wonderful, unifying worship service, bringing us together across a wide region. I also saw to it that we had greeters and hot coffee at both our usual worship sites, so we could extend hospitality to all who had chosen to worship with us that week, but who wound up at the wrong place. Win-win. Team first. Trust strengthened.

One might assume that a high degree of trust would come easier in smaller congregations. I have not found this to be the case at all. In fact, research has shown that lack of trust between members, often with a small group of members holding disproportionate power, correlates with an inability for a church to assimilate new people.

HABIT 7. FLEXIBLE ALIGNMENT

A high degree of trust leads to a heightened capacity for flexible alignment. This is a balance, calibrated slightly differently in each church, where ministries are able to adapt and innovate within a certain range of necessity and missional prudence. Most of the following examples are large multisite churches. They grew large, in part, because they practiced flexible alignment. However, in each case, as these churches grew larger, they also grew smaller, mastering the art of small venue gatherings and intimate faith community.

Life.Church (formerly LifeChurch.tv),[92] based in Oklahoma City, is now one of the largest congregations in America, with two kinds of campuses: (1) Some are highly conforming local outlets with an almost identical product from one to the next, whether you visit them in Iowa or in Pennsylvania. (2) Others are independently organized churches that choose to affiliate with them. These are able to utilize various LifeChurch resources. They are committed to conforming to a list of minimum qualifications, mostly procedural covenants, and, of course, a commitment to use the senior pastor's sermons each Sunday.

In some of the most extensive multisite ventures in the United States and across the world, there is a high degree of theological and logistical similarity from campus to campus—to the point that franchise is not too strong a word in describing things. I think of Hillsong Church, scattered across the globe, with a central financing system fueled in large part by music sales and royalties. This structural financial dependency of each campus upon the central movement leadership (holding the purse strings) lends to much control and conformity regarding certain things. Hillsong is not just multisite but multiethnic and global in its reach. Thus it is probably a wise move on their part to keep to a common script in

92. See www.life.church.

many areas of their church's life—even as they allow different preaching pastors to develop local constituencies, rather than depending on a video-venue approach to worship. They are multivalent enough to become global, but only to a point that enables stability as the church grows.[93]

The central question for any church seeking flexible alignment: how can we hold together as a unified movement, while allowing the cultural and contextual variables to inform somewhat differing ministry strategies in each place? It is, in some respects, the same question that a denomination asks, except a congregation usually keeps a tighter common life than most denominations.

On the other end of the flexibility spectrum, Christ the King Community Church, based in Burlington, Washington, has thousands of worshipers scattered across Washington state and beyond, but each campus has considerable autonomy in terms of local strategies, such as whether they own space or rent, and what kinds of specialty ministries may emerge in a particular place. Pastors preach what they want to preach each week, and more than a thousand small groups keep a wide variety of agendas and curricula. The church gives this kind of freedom in part because they are mostly white, small-town people sharing a conservative Baptist theology and a commitment to very simple church organization (worship and small group), with campus pastors who keep a very tight camaraderie.

A smaller ministry system that has practiced flexible alignment would be the Acts Network, a consortium of gatherings ranging from ten to a hundred persons, in connection to First United

93. Some would categorize Hillsong as a denomination. I think of it as a global multisite church. You could make a case for either designation.

Methodist Church of Williamsport, Pennsylvania.[94] The Acts Network groups meet in homes and other community gathering spaces. Nothing feels franchise at all from one gathering to the next, but their core values and mission shine through in each expression of faith community. Acts Network teaches us that even microcommunities can live out the promise of a connected ministry dispersed across a broad geography and a diverse demographic.

Areas where multivalent churches may allow flexibility, within a context of overall alignment, may include:

- tactical considerations in a stewardship drive;
- development of a specialized ministry, small business, or leader development process that is distinctive to a particular subcommunity within the larger church;
- certain kinds of valence that are specialized within a particular ministry department or campus and not generalized to the whole church;
- and anything experimental or innovative.

HABIT 8. THE LIMITS OF OUR VALENCE

In all multivalent churches, there is a limit to how far the ministry can stretch at any given moment without being destabilized and inadvertently blowing things up! The senior pastor and the lead team must constantly monitor the degree to which the church can (and should) be stretched.

---

94. Mitch Marcello is leader of the Acts Network. He is a layperson. Matt Lake is senior pastor of First UMC in Williamsport. I have coached them as a team—and they exemplified a great many of the positive teaming habits that we consider in this chapter.

Oversight includes responding appropriately when team members or leaders function like loose electrons: unaligned theologically, in terms of vision, or simply with the tasks of holding together a complex church. Loose electrons that are not constructively engaged in bonding will act to repel, to exert energy that pushes atoms apart from one another rather than pulling them together. This wreaks havoc and weakens the molecule. In the church, every leader must be in the game, working with the team. Covalent bonding is essential for multi churches, especially in leadership.

Loose electrons by nature have incentive to bond with something. It is just that they can find no place to bond within the current molecule. Dealing with loose electrons in love may mean helping them to find their way to another molecule (church) where they can be more constructively engaged in supporting what is being built.

What is the maximum stable valence for a single congregation? It is hard to say—but once a church is juggling five or six different kinds of multi, it may make sense to focus on getting better at existing valences before trying to layer on yet another challenge. There is no prize for extreme multivalence; however, there may be unnecessary crisis.

QUICK CHECK—HOW'S OUR TEAM DOING?

(Answer "Yes" or "No" to each question. It is recommended that a team complete this separately and then compare notes together.)

1. Does our team spend at least an hour a week in some sort of spiritual practice beyond leading a worship service for the larger church?

2. Do we pass the leadership of this time around, so that we are able to experience the perspectives and gifts of each person around the table?
3. Does our team have a covenant specifying specific commitments that we ask from everyone? Has it been updated in the last year? (Both subquestions must be "Yes" in order for this question to count as "Yes.")
4. When team members wander outside the bounds of our covenant, does something appropriate happen? (If there is no covenant, this is a "No.")
5. Can our team clearly articulate the specific ways that we are seeking to live into multivalence in our life together?
6. Does the make-up of our church's most visible leadership reflect the range of people that our church is seeking to serve?
7. Do you personally feel like the church's central management team understands you and works with you flexibly so that ministry can thrive?
8. Is there a balance between the people who move on to new ministry challenges (in other places or churches) and those who stay for a decade or more? (Too many long tenures or short tenures, without a good mix, can be sign of trouble.)
9. Do people with long tenures respond with openness to the insights and ideas of newer team members?
10. Do we try enough new things at our church? Have we started a major new ministry in the past two years?
11. When the team meets, does everyone get enough time to speak?
12. Does the team get enough relational time to keep a good sense of trust for one another?

7

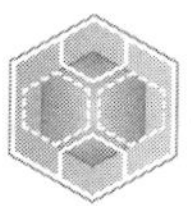

THE POSSIBILITIES

In this book we have looked briefly at the metaphor of multivalence to explore how local churches can build bridges and navigate well the complexities of the twenty-first century. We have explored varied ways churches with a relatively homogeneous heritage can adapt and thrive in a century of unprecedented challenge. Even though most churches will not embrace the changes that are required, many will do so. And they will discover ministry renaissance as a result. Multi practices, capacities, and teaming habits will enable a certain set of congregations to thrive far into the coming years, even as all the denominations downsize and some pass away entirely.

It is truly possible for churches to discover fruitfulness in these weather conditions.

Among the adaptors, the nature of their multivalence will grow more complex and sophisticated over time. Significant and ongoing change will be required in every place.

Net gains in the numbers of participants and in financial income will materialize, but it will be harder work than before.

And the gains made in one decade may dissipate in the next! Plenty of aging and expensive church buildings will be jettisoned along the way to midcentury. Yet multiple good ways forward will remain, with or without those buildings, for any band of spiritual pilgrims who are up for a robust—and multi—journey!

Plus, thousands of new multi churches will be born in the years ahead. I expect that the majority the North Americans who participate in a church in the year 2050 will do so in a church that does not yet exist!

This hope is more than enough to keep me going week unto week as I bounce from D.C. to California to Michigan to Germany and so on, encouraging local churches to rethink what they are doing. I will leave the work of closing churches for others—as for me, I stand by the thesis of my 2006 book, *I Refuse to Lead a Dying Church*.

But the multi journey is more than a strategy for church survival—so much more! Indeed, it will help a remnant of vital churches to weather tough ministry conditions. But there are greater possibilities before us—possibilities that we could easily miss, especially if our primary motivation is just to make ministry work in our existing congregations. In these final pages, I wish to mention just a few of these possibilities.

MOVEMENT AND PILGRIMAGE

During the last 150 years, Christianity in America has been slowly settling down. Add in the rising median age of American congregations (and the people within the congregations), and the United States is seeing church decline commensurate with what Europe saw two generations ago. A lot of folks think this is the lead story today for American Christianity. I disagree. It is a sobering story, but it should not be the lead story.

The shift to a multi approach counters the story of settling, declining church in significant ways. Each one of the multi capacities we have explored lends itself to movement—movement that promises the possibility of life beyond the imminent collapse of church-as-usual and of denomination. All multi capacities invite us toward a journey of transformation. This t-word, fashionable in certain church development circles these days, is simply a synonym for the c-word: change. Serious change. Change: the opposite of sitting still, of settling. To aspire toward a multi kind of life, churches are choosing to change, to gird up, to pack lightly, and to be people on a journey—people letting go of status quo and living into newness.

Multivalent churches unsettle things and nudge us back into the movement zone. This can only be good news for the future of faith in America—in a moment when too little good news is heard.

Multisite churches have been associated with church growth during a season when church as usual has seen historic decline. The same is soon to be true of multiethnic churches. Multi churches are the islands of hope and ministry innovation in a sea of prolific numerical decline. Multi is a movement rooted in the vitality of the local in all of its beautiful diversity. Not only do multi churches run on local energy, in many cases they are able to create regional zones of healthy ministry DNA and to mentor churches toward an alternative horizon of hope that feels entirely different than the culture of institutional preservation and death that surrounds them.[95]

95. The culture of death in denominations arises simply from the cumulative effects of so many congregations declining and aging out all at once, further aggravated by the culture wars playing out in American society. As the churches decline and their money dries up, the denominational judicatory itself is endangered. This feeds the current obsession with church metrics, as if more aggressive measuring will somehow create a less discouraged clergy, erase decades of social change, and inspire a different kind of church.

Because the vitality is largely local, judicatory leaders of declining systems may at times choose to perceive such vitality as a threat to their power. I watched one Methodist district superintendent dismantle and destroy a rising multisite church. Granted, this is not the norm in my experience of judicatory leaders, but presiding over a culture of dying churches can skew one's perspective. When almost everything we manage is in decline, and then something thrives beyond our control, we may feel threatened.

Multiethnic churches represent a new possibility for congregational life that has eluded settled churches throughout American history. Multilingual and multinarrative churches represent hopeful possibilities for building relationship and spiritual partnership with doggedly postmodern people, few of whom will ever again engage their parents' church. Multitheological churches exist across the spectrum from evangelical to Unitarian, and when they cobble together coalitions of diverse theological outlook artfully, they often see growth.[96]

At every turn, multi upends the status quo of the settled American church. If you have a vested interest in that status quo as a context for consolidating personal power, either as an episcopal candidate or as a ruling patriarch of a local church, you may want to fight against multi—because it could upend you. But I would say to status quo guardians the same thing I say to the church planters that I coach: Show up to whatever God is doing in your neighborhood—show up humbly, with a Bible, a broom, and a dustpan. Show up to serve, to join the Spirit movement that God

96. Unitarian Universalist churches are growing in America, one of the rare denominations posting net gains. In my view, this is because of UU appeal to a spiritual pilgrim mentality.

started without you—and therein you will discover the pathway to ministry blessing and to a fruitful life.

A PLACE BEYOND POLARIZATION AND SCHISM

The same core practices that undergird us in our readiness to do multi well at the local church level also equip us for a different kind of engagement with one another at the level of the network or denomination. The abilities to pray contemplatively and to listen deeply to one another increase our ability to articulate together the things that engage, energize, and unite us. We need this kind of capacity beyond the local! We need this in the wider church life and also within our political life.

Schism is not always a bad thing; sometimes it helps to create constructive space between parties who are wasting too much energy in opposition to each other. One of the reasons that many denominations often get along well with each other these days is because their fights over theology and polity were fought so long ago—resulting in the creation of organizational space between each another, enabling each to live out their faith without a sense of threat from other churches. Generations later, they no longer pose a threat to each other, even when they disagree. They are able to collaborate when doing so serves their common advantage, and not to collaborate when it doesn't.

That neighbor who drinks too much at your parties but who always goes home across the expanse of green between your house and his—if you lived with him it would be a fight all the time. But, with a little space, he remains a good friend across the years. Sometimes a little space makes all the difference! The chairperson of my church council used to say, "The most beautiful Christmas lights are the lights on the back of the car, as my kids pull out of the driveway to go home after Christmas." (And he dearly loved his children!)

Trying to live together beneath one roof, organizationally, is not always the best way forward. Every bold move by one party threatens somebody else within the organization—promising dull moderation, constant conflict, or both! The loosening of structural ties may reduce the sense of threat that certain people pose to others. With the threat reduced, both innovation and collaboration become easier—in serving our neighbors and in offering a common witness to the gospel.

In multi kinds of churches, as we deal with more than one way to worship, or to articulate our salvation stories, or to serve different neighborhoods, the ministry itself can train us to move beyond binary thinking. For every question that has a hard and defined answer, there are so many others that are largely matters of context. Doing multi well requires clarity in each church as to which questions are which. Multi ministries are bound by rather tight consensus on some questions, even as they differ on other questions. It is through the intimacy of relationship with those whose stories and life experiences challenge ours that we grow to appreciate the approaches to ministry that bless others, even when it might not be our cup of tea. Similarly, sometimes being a multi church becomes easier when it just doesn't have to all happen under one physical roof. Watching our sisters and brothers go to their campus (across the green so to speak) may help us stay constructively connected! For the people we are not yet reaching, offering them a constructive option without forcing them into our traditional space opens up doors of connection.

With the increasing diversity (and the acrimony) of modern life, life is fast propelling us toward a way of seeing life and one another that is more gracious and peace-filled. Multi churches can be gifts to all of us, helping to set the conditions where we might move beyond the demonizing of our neighbors. Beth Estock would remind us that the survival of the planet increasingly depends on enlarging our capacity for seeing one another with empathy. The stakes are high—more than simply restoring civility in local community life or to Thanksgiving dinner tables. We will profit by a significant increase of persons seeing the both/and of the world in all sorts of community contexts: churches, neighborhoods, businesses, and political parties.

RENEWED SENSE OF INDIGENOUS

The Christian gospel, or "good news," is amazingly multicultural. It grew out of a historic context at a crossroads between the three major continents of the earth. The original cultural context is long past; Christianity in its essence is no longer African or European. Neither Asian nor American. Even though it emerged in the first century, it transcends that time, having been reborn in multiple revivals across the centuries on every continent except Antarctica.

One of the best examples of how Christianity can be culturally embedded in a new place without losing its essence is Vincent Donovan's tale of his work as a Catholic missionary in east Africa more than a century ago. Donovan worked to learn the language, then the culture. He discovered that an entirely new atonement metaphor was needed, and he went on to develop it based on his understanding of the local culture. After many years of patient faith dialogue, suddenly everything came together, and nearly all the Maasai people were able to make sense of God's grace, as we know it from the biblical tradition. And they became Christian within a few weeks.[97] But they did not become European Catholics. They became Maasai Christians—with a Christian faith rooted deeply in the instincts and categories of their lives.

Throughout the centuries of Christian mission, we have constantly dealt with the human propensity to attach our cultural baggage to Jesus. Often, we have lost clarity of where Jesus stops and our baggage starts—it all blurs together. Too often we have exported more than Christian faith, bundling the gospel with aspects of culture and tradition that are not essential to Christianity. In some cases, we have attached stuff that honestly is not even compatible with the spirit of Christianity! When we do this, our faith becomes a pretext for expanding our own influence, politics, and power in the world. We call this colonialism. It is an ever present danger, any time we share our faith with the world, that we tend to package it in ways that ask people to buy in to more than simply the good news at the heart of Christianity. At times, the package presented may undermine the fullness of the good news that our faith has to offer a community, missing major aspects of the gospel that are important and relevant to the neighborhood where we are working.

In the 1500s Christian colonialism meant that Christianity entered the Americas in collusion with the Spanish empire. Dominican friars accompanied Spanish explorer Tristan de Luna. They celebrated the first Christian mass on (what is today) U.S. soil at Pensacola Beach, Florida, August 15, 1559. It happened just across the street from the condo where I used to live. On my early morning beach walks, I used to find that place to be a thin space

97. Vincent Donovan, *Christianity Rediscovered* (Chicago: Fides/Claretian Press, 1978).

of beauty and divine mystery. But let's be clear—it was a mass for armed soldiers who had stepped onto that lovely white sand beach for the purpose of extending the Spanish empire into the Americas. The missionaries and the empire were in total collusion.

Christianity has brought spiritual blessing to untold millions of people. Yet with this blessing came centuries of economic and cultural oppression and institutionalized poverty. Similar tales could be shared relative to much of European and American missionary work. Part of the early resistance to Christianity in China was directly related to the ways that western cultural norms and political domination of Asia were connected to the introduction of Christian faith. Had Chinese Christianity not been tied to western colonialism, one can only wonder if the pushback of the Cultural Revolution in the 1960s would have unfolded with such trauma and persecution. After the 1960s, however, Christianity reemerged as a more indigenous movement in China—with entirely home-grown leaders, and they've arguably outdone even the apostles of the first century in terms of the sheer force of the movement, with perhaps 150 million Christian believers, reached in about half a century.

With such complex Christian history, a church with high valence should take great care when crossing socioeconomic, cultural, and ethnic lines, seeking to build local ministry teams in each place that reflect the people who live there. If a church's constituency represents a focused demographic scattered across various neighborhoods, it might make sense to go to a multisite video-venue plan where the same sermon from the same person occurs in each worship venue. This is efficient and keeps the campuses on the same page. However, if there is a significant population difference between neighborhoods or a longing for high authenticity and personal touch, it makes more sense to rely on a live campus pastor who can help to present the faith in ways that are relevant to and honoring of the local neighborhood cultures.

The more diverse the people gathered in any place, the more that the plan and the leadership must reflect that diversity. The more multivalent a church is, the greater chance that we will have the kinds of leaders within the church already who are suited to help develop new ministries for new people. When a church sees that it lacks the full range of leaders needed for ministry to a new demographic, a higher multivalence will help the church to grasp the challenge and to onboard some new team members. When the furtherance of the mission requires letting campuses or ministries spin off as new congregations entirely, a multi church is more apt to understand the right timing—and to see this independence as a step forward and not a failure.

A PUBLIC FAITH IN A POST–CHRISTENDOM CULTURE

In the first two centuries of American history, Christendom sensibilities meant not only legislating certain notions of Christian morality but also structuring society in a way that leaned toward justice for the least powerful people. Along with the concern for personal evangelism, there was profound social concern focused on building a society in line with a good and godly vision for human life. This social concern expressed itself on a variety of fronts and in a variety of forms. It fueled the movement for public education. It created hundreds of charitable institutions to help people in all sorts of ways. It basically invented mass public health care. It sped up the movement for the abolition of slavery. It also gave us Prohibition in the 1920s. In the late 1950s, it clung tightly to the American Civil Rights movement, keeping it rooted deeply as a biblically based movement, with thousands of American churches organizing for justice.

With the significant decline in the church's political power in the last half century, what was once a broad movement has now splintered into two movements on the opposite fringes of church life. On one end, the justice warriors, still pushing for a more inclusive world, focus these days on eliminating police violence against black lives, giving equal rights to transgender persons, and fighting for the human dignity of undocumented American residents. On the other end we have the culture warriors, working hard to bring back some vestige of their perception of Christendom. The majority of American Christians are not deeply connected to either movement. In the broad middle, we have a church in America where faith has been largely focused on helping us in our personal lives. Too often, we are cut off from the larger questions of our life together—perhaps because our politics has become so polarized and churches don't want to drag political acrimony into our spiritual experience.

Christendom culture has ended in most parts of the world, with the possible exception of a few rural counties in the American heartland—and a few other places around the planet where the church structures have remained deeply enmeshed with political power. By Christendom, we mean a culture where church and public life are deeply intermixed. In that world gone by, almost everyone understands himself or herself as Christian by virtue of citizenship. There is little distinction between church laws and secular laws. So any moral concern that is rooted in one's Christian faith is automatically a concern for public life and law. In this world, persons who are other-than-Christian (as the majority interprets Christian) are viewed with suspicion and expected to accept lesser status.

In United States, a shrinking group of people grieves for a world lost, taking their grief out on everybody else. These grieving ones are a subset of the total Christian population, which is also shrinking. Most Christians that I know sincerely want to take their faith beyond their personal lives to honor God in the wider sphere. This wider action consists largely of mainstream charitable work, to love those who have been hit with misfortunes of natural disasters, poverty, or being orphaned. So far, so good! However, this action can also emerge as efforts to legislate a certain understanding of morality into law, forcing others to conform to rules and practices rooted in one particular type of Christianity.

The culture warriors are sprinkled about in many of our churches—and they represent some of the best among us, even if they choose to fight quixotic battles. Sometimes, their efforts are labeled as hate speech, due to the pain they inflict in the lives of their neighbors (gay, Muslim, or simply secular). Hate organizations are real. But honestly, in my experience—working in hundreds of heartland churches across the last three decades—our more conservative folks are more lovers than haters. They simply are doing what seems sensible to them in terms of living a faithful life.

The current dance of faith and politics will likely fade considerably in the United States by midcentury as the number of white evangelical and Catholic Christians dips below the point where they will be able to wield as much political power. While this may strike some as a very sad prognosis for the future, I am hopeful that it will give way to a more constructive type of civic engagement for people of faith.

Christianity typically functions better from a minority status in the larger society. When Jesus said that the people of God's realm are the salt of the earth, he was saying that a few of us are able to make a big difference in terms of seasoning a much larger society. John Wesley talked about reforming the nation and spreading scriptural holiness across the land. Wesley was a child of Christendom, but his movement was often at odds with the settled state religion of England. I love the image of spreading scriptural holiness across a land. It feels in sync with Jesus's vision of God's realm. But as a minority people, we must recognize that political power grabs are dangerous for us (they go to our head), dangerous for our witness (they brand us as power grabbers and control freaks), and dangerous for the world (they cut people off from being able to appreciate the gospel message due to the distastefulness of the messenger).

A multi church is more likely to see that...

- Followers of Jesus have differing political philosophies that grow from their respective life experiences. Because they choose to work across lines of diversity, they are acutely aware that there are multiple Christian answers to any political question. None of us has the perfect answers.
- Listening to one another, hearing each other's stories, is critical—it is not only the foundation of church life in a multi context, it offers a critical practice for a workable civic life.
- A servant people, who live to bless their neighbors, will be received (by the neighbors) very differently than a conquering people, who live to control their neighbors.
- Sometimes it's wise to compromise our personal preferences in order to build something beautiful with our neighbors. The discovery of a beautiful *us* is more fulfilling than a beautiful *me*.
- Loving neighbor as oneself is a big deal—an ideal that transcends Christian faith. The spirit of loving neighbor as oneself offers a great foundation for creating laws and political

structures. While we may disagree on what loving neighbor as oneself may look like in the political arena, just advocating for this principle as a core foundation and motivation in civic life is an advance over the current acrimony.

- Anything that impedes neighbors listening to neighbors is getting in the way of a society that can bless the most people. This includes the unregulated flood of money from big corporations into the political conversation, which arguably has done more to stifle the art of civil civic conversation than any other particular thing.
- The aftermath of slavery must be overcome and healed. Churches represent one of our best avenues for such healing. The fact that black and white voters live in such different worlds, almost two centuries after Emancipation, is proof that we have a lot of unfinished work in healing racism. There is a connection between segregation in our churches and segregation in the ways we vote. Those who transcend the old boundaries of race and class bring a different perspective to political questions. They may still lean left or right, but their perspective is less animated by fear of the other, or in anger toward the other. They are also able to see some wisdom in what the other is saying and to express some empathy in the other's experience.
- As we grow a more multi church in America, we will develop leaders who can convene the kinds of conversations, the kinds of relationships, that are necessary for healing the layers of misunderstanding that exist between black and white, between left and right, between indigenous and immigrant, and so on.

- And from understanding, there comes the possibility of reconciliation, with integrity and with appropriate justice—and a renewed opportunity for the American political experiment to work!

A RENEWED WITNESS

Those who have left organized church very often see the church more as part of the problem(s) than as part of the solution(s). A multi church represents a way forward that puts the church on a higher moral ground—in ways that persons of an emerging worldview can appreciate. A church that is clearly a leader in the healing of our world (socially, economically, ecologically) will have a strong future if that church is also committed to embrace its Christological core.

One of the reasons that I joined The United Methodist Church back in the 1980s was that it represented the best attempt I had yet seen at bringing liberals and evangelicals into one fellowship. I still love the Methodists for this, even as I work with churches of various traditions. And yet, the UMC has come upon difficult times in terms of its search for a way forward to continue as a denomination of such diversity. Most likely, it will split into two or more denominations. To my church, and to all the churches with whom I work, I would offer this appeal:

The best way forward is not a purification campaign that runs out all of the people who disagree with us or see life from a different experience than us! That is a way backward. Furthermore, the best way forward can never fully be realized at the level of high-altitude denominational structures, policies, and negotiations. I do not want to discourage those who are called to lead and to negotiate for a workable unity at the level of the denomination—I pray for your success! But I also know that the dust always settles after denominational mergers, schisms, and reconciliations. And we have to get back to doing ministry in the places that we call church.

The most critical church vitality is always local. The best hope for church renewal is local. Young people are won to faith and confirmed locally. Disciples are made locally. Mission happens at a particular time, at a particular locale. Would-be pastors experience their calls to ministry locally, and they are endorsed to begin a journey into pastoral leadership first by their local churches. The worship most likely to change people's lives: it happens locally, week after week after week in a neighborhood context. Even Jesus's most basic work was to nurture a *local* circle of disciples into a team of world-changers. He constantly ducked the temptation and invitation to spend his time working at a macro level. He knew that unless the gospel could be embedded within that local circle of apostles, nothing world-changing could ever occur. Without local church vitality, even the best and most renewed denominational structures and collaborative endeavors slowly fade away.

Leveraging the power and healthy DNA of vital local churches is our best way forward as a Christian movement in America. It is the best way to plant anything new that will thrive—and it is the best way to renew denominational movements—or to create new movements that live past those whose time has come and gone.

When a local circle of diverse spiritual friends can live into God's vision for humanity on a micro scale, there is hope for all the rest of us! The gospel moves from theory and vision into reality first within a local circle. And it will often spread like wildfire from there. It can't sit still. It certainly can't be contained within a sanctuary, or within a set demographic. It spreads.

The gospel goes multi.

The gospel always seems to go multi.